NEPAD at Country Level - Changing Aid Relationships in Tanzania

Edited by
Samuel M. Wangwe

MKUKI NA NYOTA PUBLISHERS
DAR ES SALAAM

Published for the Economic and Social Research Foundation
by Mkuki na Nyota Publishers
6 Muhonda St., Mission Quarter, Kariakoo
P.O. Box 4246, Dar es Salaam

ISBN 9987-686-28-1

Distributed outside Africa by
African Books Collective Ltd
27 Park end Street
Oxford OX1 1HU
UK

CONTENTS

FOREWORD

Tanzania has been a partner in development cooperation since the 1960s and over time the relationship between the partners has been evolving. The most dramatic period in the evolution of aid relationships between Tanzania and its development partners occurred between 1995 and 2000, and it is still continuing. This volume documents developments in aid relationships in development cooperation between Tanzania and its donors during this critical period. The evolution of the process of reform and monitoring of aid relationships is still in progress, based on this experience. The publication of this volume will make it possible for a wider audience to have access to this experience. It is believed that the lessons emerging from this experience will be relevant to other countries, which are undergoing the process of redefining new partnerships in development cooperation.

Tanzania was one of the major beneficiaries of aid in Africa in the 1970s and 1980s. Over the period, the amount of aid and the number of donors operating in Tanzania has been rising. The relationship in the 1970s was relatively balanced, with foreign aid filling the investment-savings, and the foreign exchange gaps. Donors responded to Tanzania's requirements in most cases based on the conviction that Tanzania's development philosophy and development agenda were basically in the right direction. The policies pursued and the development agenda were not questioned by the donors.

The situation started to change in the early 1980s when the Bretton Wood Institutions (BWIs) started to question Tanzania's basic economic policy framework asserting that domestic policies and domestic economic mismanagement were the main causes of the economic crisis. Tanzania authorities on the other hand were pointing to the external factors (e.g. deteriorating terms of trade, the oil crisis, war with Idi Amin's Uganda, collapse of the East African Community) for the explanation of the crisis. The debate broadened and brought on board several other donors on the side of the BWIs. By 1985 most donors were convinced that domestic policies in Tanzania needed to change for aid to be effective. Many of them cut back on aid until the policy stance changed in 1986 when Tanzania reached an agreement with the BWIs. In the second half of the 1980s donors resumed aid flows to Tanzania but this time round aid was tied to policy reforms. The relationship had changed from one in which Tanzania owned its policies in the 1970s to one in which the policy agenda was largely driven by the BWIs with donor's support.

In the early 1990s both sides were getting dissatisfied with each other. Donors were developing the feeling that aid was not being effective while the Tanzania side was increasingly feeling that donors were exerting undue influence on the policy reform process. The deteriorating aid relationships culminated in the action by donors to reduce aid flows in 1992-94 period on the grounds that the Tanzania government was failing to collect revenue including counterpart funds from import support programmes. Donors perceived inefficient administration, budget mismanagement and corruption on the part of Tanzania. The Tanzania government blamed the donors for making unrealistic and excessive demands on Tanzania and interfering excessively in the policy reform process while unable to deliver on the promises made regarding resource inflows. At the height of the deteriorating relations the Danish government, in agreement with the Tanzania government, funded an independent group of five experts led by Professor Gerry Helleiner of the University of Toronto to address the deteriorating aid relationships from three perspectives: aid effectiveness, global trends in aid flows and macroeconomic performance. The others were Prof. Benno Ndulu (Tanzania), Prof. Nguyuru Lipumba (Tanzania), Prof. Tony Killick (UK) and Prof. Knud Erik Svendsen (Denmark). The point that stands out in the whole report is that ownership of projects; programmes and policies had been eroded considerably.

The group delivered the report in June 1995 with 21 recommendations for both the Tanzania government and the donors. This report, popularly known as *The Helleiner Report* was taken up by the Third Phase Government (from November 1995). The Mkapa government put high on its agenda the challenge of restoring healthy aid relationships. In 1996 the Tanzania government met with the Nordic countries on how aid relationships could best be restored using *The Helleiner Report* as a major input. The agreement with the Nordic countries in September 1996 paved the way for a broader discussion with the donor community at a workshop held in

Dar es Salaam in January 1997. *The Helleiner Report* was the main point of discussion. The main outcome of the workshop was agreement on the major steps to be taken by both sides to start a new aid relationship. The guiding principle was ownership and leadership by Tanzania in policy and development cooperation. Specifically, 16 steps to be taken were agreed upon and a follow up mechanism was agreed upon. Progress made was to be a subject of subsequent Consultative Group (CG) meetings. Reporting of progress made was led by Helleiner at the CG meetings in December 1997, 1999 and May 2000. The independent assessment of performance that Prof. Helleiner made was in each case discussed frankly and openly by both Parties (Tanzania government and donors) and agreement was reached on areas where action was needed.

At the CG meeting of 1999 it was agreed, in principle, that the on-going process of independent monitoring of aid relationships needed to be institutionalised. This was followed by preparation of a Tanzania Assistance Strategy (2000) to govern the on-going relationship between the Tanzania government and its development partners. At the CG meeting in 2000 it was agreed that the implementation of TAS would include independent monitoring and evaluation of donor performance as well as Tanzanian performance. Since then the Economic and Social Research Foundation (ESRF), an independent not-for-profit NGO, has been appointed to work as an honest broker coordinating the independent monitoring with donor funding coordinated by the UNDP. The Independent Monitoring Group consists of two Tanzanians (Prof. S. Wangwe as overall Coordinator and Amb. Fadhili Mmbaga), three experts from donor countries (Prof. Tony Killick of UK, Prof. Rolf Hofmeier of Germany and Mr. Goran Anderson of Sweden) and one African non-Tanzanian (Mr. Emmanuel Tumusiime Mutebile of Uganda). All the members of the IMG were selected on the basis of their independence from the Tanzania government and from the donor administrations. The work of the IMG commenced in February 2002 and the report is to be presented to the 2002 CG meeting. All parties are committed to supporting the IMG work up to end of 2003 after which the situation is to be reviewed in view of the experience which will have been gained.

The current volume is a unique documentation of the process of addressing the aid relationships between Tanzania government and donors. It contains main milestones in this process. Starting with *The Helleiner Report* (1995) it also includes the lead paper by Prof. Samuel Wangwe, which contains comments, and observations, which were made on *The Helleiner Report* at the joint workshop in January 1997, and the 16 points which were agreed upon at the end of the workshop. The workshop agreements were followed up by independent assessments which were presented for discussion at subsequent CG meetings in December 1997, May 1999 and May 2000. These assessments are included in this volume.

This volume also contains a most comprehensive record of the process of reform of aid relationships in Tanzania. The evolution of the process of reforming and monitoring the aid relationships has in many ways been characterised-by-learning by doing. While the process is bound to evolve further, this volume documents the rather unique Tanzanian experience in reforming and monitoring aid relationships and pioneering the evolution a new partnership in development cooperation. Discussions about the desirability of new partnerships in development have drawn attention within the donor community (e.g. within OECD – DAC) and within Africa as expressed in the New Partnership for African Development (NEPAD). What has yet to be documented adequately are country experiences of what the evolution towards this new partnership could be. This volume is expected to contribute to filling this gap. The lessons emerging from this experience are in many ways pioneering and stand out as a major contribution to giving concrete meaning to the development of a new partnership in development cooperation.

Professor S. M. Wangwe
Executive Director, ESRF
Dar es Salaam, February 2002

PREFACE

The Group of Independent Advisers on Development Cooperation Issues between Tanzania and its Aid Donors was formed in mid-1994 at the initiative of the Ministry of Foreign Affairs of the government of Denmark. The final membership of the group was as follows: Gerald K. Helleiner (Chairman), Department of Economics, University of Toronto; Tony Killick, Overseas Development Institute, London; Benno J. Ndulu, African Economic Research Consortium and University of Dar es Salaam; Nguyuru Lipumba based in Dar es Salaam; and Knud Erik Svendsen, Centre for Development Research, Copenhagen. Its original membership included John F. Toye of the Institute of Development Studies, University of Sussex, who was forced to withdraw because of other commitments early in 1995 and was replaced by Tony Killick.

The terms of reference agreed between the Government of Denmark and the government of Tanzania were as follows:

I. The general objective of the task of the group will be to assess whether the development cooperation between the Government of Tanzania (GoT) and the official donor organisations could be strengthened in order to realise the economic and social development objectives agreed between GoT and the donor community in the best possible way.

II. Based on frank and open discussions with representatives of the GoT and major donors, and perhaps other sources of information as well, the group is invited to form its own independent views on how cooperation efforts could be made more efficient.

Particular attention should be given to constraints which in the opinion of the group could be reduced or removed by GoT, the donors, or by the partners in common.

III. As a minimum the assessment shall address the following issues:

1. The efficiency and relevance of the current dialogue between GoT and donor community regularly taking place both inside and outside Tanzania.

2. The relevance and effectiveness of the totality of aid programmes, including the modes, composition and administration of cooperation (programme aid, project aid, technical assistance, etc.); conditionalities, donor cooperation,

absorption capacity of the Tanzanian economy and the institutions through which the aid is channeled; and problems of accountability.

In the assessment of the issues under (1) and (2) above, the group shall consider what should be understood, in the Tanzanian situation, by the concept of 'ownership', now widely accepted as a cornerstone in the relationships between African countries and their donors.

At the end of the assignment, the group shall produce a report for the GoT and its official donors, which contains the group's proposals.

The full group met for two days in Copenhagen in September 1994, two days in Washington, DC in November 1994, seven days in Dar es Salaam in March-April 1995, and again for another day in Washington in May 1995. Subgroups of its members also met with individual donors and attended the Tanzania Consultative Group meeting in Paris in February 1995.

The report is unanimous. Each member of the group assumes full responsibility for the entire text.

We should like to thank all those who gave us their time and their thoughts. We were honoured by the honesty and frankness with which we were received both within the Government of Tanzania and throughout the donor community. We should particularly like to thank Fulgence Kazaura, Secretary of the Planning Commission, and Dr Enos S. Bukuku, of the Prime Minister's office, for their facilitation of our contacts and discussions with officials of the Government of Tanzania. We are also most grateful to Ole Moelgaard Andersen, Mark Jensen and Ambassador Flemming Bjoerk Pedersen, of the Government of Denmark, without whom this effort would not have been possible. We hope that all those who contributed to our efforts will conclude that their assistance was justified.

Chapter 1

Development Cooperation Issues Between Tanzania and Its Aid Donors

Report of the Group of Independent Advisors

by Gerald K. Helleiner (Chairman)
Tony Killick, Nguyuru Lipumba, Benno J.
Ndulu and Knud Erik Svendsen

Report of the Group of Independent Advisers

1. THE CRISIS IN AID RELATIONSHIPS IN TANZANIA
1.1 The Background to the Crisis

During the course of the past year and a half, relations between the Government of Tanzania (GoT) and its principal sources of external official finance have seriously deteriorated. The prospects for continuing economic, social and political progress in Tanzania(are continuing economic, social; and political in Tanzania) are now clouded by an unprecedented degree of tension between the GoT and its principal aid donors.

The recent difficulties are seen by many to originate with the longstanding failure of the GoT to collect, as agreed, all of the counterpart funds arising from donors' import support programmes. These arrears, which generated suspicions of corruption and have still not been fully dealt with, have been an important and continuing irritant to donors. Following the disappointing fiscal performance in the 1993/94 fiscal year, which led to the setting up of an IMF 'shadow' programme in the first half of 1994, Tanzania's problems were aggravated at a tense meeting between donors and the finance minister in March 1994. Donors increasingly expressed longer-term disillusionment. Their intensified concern about the effectiveness of aid to Tanzania was manifest in a series of substantial aid evaluations by the Nordic, which were initiated and completed in 1994 and discussed at a major conference in Dar es Salaam in January 1995. Our independent group on aid relationships was appointed in mid-1994.

Since then, elements of these relationships have become even more strained. Events came to a head in November 1994, at which time the newly introduced systems of information collection and disclosure generated information on tax performance and tax evasion which, in the light of previous government commitments, was sufficiently alarming to lead to a major presidential statement, the replacement of the Finance Minister, and the postponement of a planned meeting of the donor consultative Group. Plans for an ESAF programme with the IMF and a World Bank structural adjustment credit, based on an already agreed policy framework paper, both of which were at an advanced stage of preparation, were put 'on hold'. The principal donors responded by suspending their non-project finance.

The donor consultative group finally met in late February 1995, at which time donors expressed their unhappiness with Tanzania's performance in unprecedented terms. Many spoke of the loss of the previous climate of confidence' and of the reduced 'credibility of the government's commitment to reform'. In the end, the donors expressed their continued financial support for the Government of Tanzania but did so in more careful and qualified terms than previously. During the subsequent months, further overruns in the Tanzanian budget have emerged and the plans for the negotiation of a new ESAF with the IMF have again been postponed. With the current macroeconomic situation lagging behind expectations and the continuing malaise in aid relationships, the major progress of the past nine years is now at significant risk.

In the donors' view, as expressed variously to us, and caricaturing only slightly, the government of Tanzania has lost its momentum and its sense of direction, has little sense of direction, has little sense of ownership of its major programmes, and is unable to exercise fiscal control because of declining administrative capacity and increasing corruption. After more that thirty years of support, donors are disappointed with the Tanzanian performance record and regard their continued support for the GoT as politically unsustainable among their own electorates. They do not believe that the government is doing all it can in terms of revenue collection and is therefore inordinately dependent upon their aid. At the same time it is unresponsive, except in rhetoric, to donor concerns in this regard. Having lost confidence in the government's administrative and budgetary controls, donors have introduced control systems and independent ownership of programmes that were not there before. Many donors accept some responsibility, as longstanding partners, for Tanzania's failed projects and programmes. They are also frequently ambivalent about the ownership issue: some demand that the government take greater control of their programmes and at the same time resist when attempts to do so are at the expense of their own preferred projects. But they are uniform in their assignment of blame for Tanzania's current weak performance, lack of 'will' and corruption.

The GoT, on its side, considers that the donors are often unrealistic in their demands and their impatience. Its politicians and officials believe that the pace of change in Tanzania is as fast as is technically and politically feasible. They feel that they are being singled out for disproportionate (and negative) attention by the international donor community. They perceive the problem of increased corruption as, in part, a response to reduced real public sector wages and salaries; while seeking to lessen it, they see the problem as no more severe in Tanzania than in other developing countries. They regard the donors as 'driving' Tanzanian development programmes and intruding excessively upon matters of domestic policy, and they resent their inability or unwillingness to share information. They do not appreciate the donors' evident lack of trust or their consequent efforts to circumvent the government system by creating project 'islands' of their own. The key economic officials and ministers are overwhelmed by the heavy demands made by their time and energy by the requirements of economic management and reform. They are frustrated by the sheer number of frequent meetings, reports, and contacts that donors require. They argue that inappropriate and impossible donor demands may prejudice some considerable progress that they have so far managed to achieve.

The grievances of the aid donors and their concerns are genuine. So too are those of the GoT. The continuation of productive relationships between the donor community and the government requires that attempts be made squarely to address the grievances and concerns on all sides.

RECOMMENDATION 1: Both the Government of Tanzania and the major aid donors can and should initiate major changes in their relationships in order to restore mutual confidence and the prospect of continuing progress in Tanzania. Both should now be planning for a gradual decline in the degree of external support for Tanzania and reforms in the modes and processes through which it moves.

1.2 The Crisis in Context

In order fully to understand the current situation in Tanzania, it is necessary to place it into an appropriate overall context. It is also important to try to analyse the situation in an integrated fashion rather than from the perspective of the one player, whether it be the government of Tanzania or any individual donor. We therefore begin this report with some contextual and factual information.

The united Republic of Tanzania is not the only African country involved in a difficult relationship with its external sources of finance. Donors are everywhere facing budget cuts and increased pressures for the support of new countries in Eastern Europe and the former Soviet Union, Sub-Saharan Africa, and elsewhere. Moreover, disappointment with Sub Saharan African economic performance is widespread in the aid community. After so many years of support, electorates in the donor countries and the governments responsible to them, perhaps understandably, frequently suffer from 'aid fatigue'. The aid flows to Sub-Saharan Africa are therefore now universally projected to decline. The disappointments and tensions in the relationships between the GoT and its aid donors are thus growing. Perhaps because of Tanzania's prominence in the aid budgets of the Nordic countries and the Netherlands, countries noted for their excellent donor record and their previous high expectations of the Tanzania Government, the emerging difficulties in overall aid relationships in Africa seem now to be unusually focused upon the present Tanzania solution. The handling of the current Tanzania aid 'crisis' may therefore have wide ramifications far beyond those affecting only the government and people of Tanzania.

The Government of Tanzania has received significant external financial assistance ever since the country's independence in 1961; it still receives considerably more, as a percentage of its GDP, than most other African countries, although in terms of dollar receipts per capita it is only about average (see appendix Table 1)[1]

---

[1] When official development assistance is calculated as a share of recipient GDP, Tanzania appears to be an extraordinarily fortunate recipient, but this is purely the result of its very low reported – and almost certainly understated – dollar per capita income. From donor and aid – analytical perspectives, dollar receipts per capita are probably better indicators of aid directions.

In the early part of this more than thirty-year-old aid relationship, particularly in the late 1960s and 1970s, many donors were enthusiastic about the equity-oriented and socialistic aspirations of the government and the then President Julius Nyerere. The World Bank and many bilateral donors provided strong support for what seemed to be one of the most exciting and visionary of the post-independence African efforts at development.

By the late 1970s and early 1980s, however, the Tanzanian economy had run into serious macroeconomic and structural difficulties battered by external shocks and run down by policy mistakes and inherent weaknesses and inefficiencies in its own system. After a period of debate with external donors and the international financial institutions, and some initially hesitant policy change, the government finally embarked on a major programme of macroeconomic stabilisation, structural adjustment and attempted recovery, beginning in 1986. Aid, which had been cut back during the period of Tanzania's most extreme economic malaise and the dissension with the IMF and World Bank, now resumed its previous growth. The government's reliance upon aid grew rapidly once more, and the donor community became deeply involved, not least through its considerable non-project finance, in the post-1986 adjustment and recovery effort.

Tanzania is one of the relatively few countries in sub-Saharan Africa that have engaged in sustained adjustment effort with external donor support for an extended period of time—in Tanzania's case over the past nine years. It has frequently been described as a 'successful adjuster'. In a recent study by the World Bank, updating its previous widely quoted research on macroeconomic reform and growth in Africa.

And using data up to 1991-1992, Tanzania appears at one end – the upper end – of its scale. In terms of both its 'change in macroeconomic policies' and its improvement in GDP per capita growth, Tanzania is reported as performing better than any other African country. (World Bank, 'Adjustment in Africa: update on reversing economic decline in sub-Saharan Africa', findings, Africa region, No. 34, February 1995.) (The macroeconomic data thereafter will not show quite so favourable a record.) Until recently, it has also been 'on track' with a number of major structural reforms including reform in the trade and exchange regime, large-scale privatisation of para-state bodies, decontrol of prices and agricultural marketing, and retrenchment of the public service. The draft policy framework paper agreed between the GoT and the IMF and World Bank in September 1994 both acknowledged the reforms already accomplished and outlined further targets for structural reform.

Fiscal performance has been at the centre of much of the recent controversy between the GoT and the donors. We have therefore made some effort to set this performance within the context of a longer time horizon and the African experience. Has the GoT been unduly slack in its efforts to raise domestic revenues? This is not an easy question to address. Data difficulties are considerable and the results (presented in Appendix tables 2 and 3) are not unambiguous.

Government revenues as a percentage of GDP have been quite respectable in Tanzania, by African standard, and have climbed impressively since 1986. Deficits have also been low by African standards, better than such other 'successful' adjusters as Ghana and Uganda (Appendix Table 2). However, these data may overstate Tanzanian performance, if its GDP is relatively understated and/or if that relative understatement is increasing; both are possible. Aware that there are also major problems surrounding the choice of exchange rates for conversion of local currencies into dollars, we nevertheless compared Tanzanian government revenues per capita in dollar terms, exclusive of grants, with others, as a check. On this measure, the Tanzanian record does not look quite so impressive. Its revenue performance is still much better, however, than that of Uganda (Appendix Table 3). We conclude that there is no clear basis for singling out Tanzania as particularly lacking in revenue effort, although we still have many critical comments to make about the GoT's performance in this regard. (We also make recommendations to the GoT concerning its appropriate response to more detailed complaints of donors in sections 3 and 4.)

Despite the fact that aggregate output is now growing more rapidly and recent expenditure surveys indicate that actual GDP may be twice as large as the current official estimate, over 40 per cent of the population continue to live below the absolute poverty level. The government's earlier concern with broad based development has been little in evidence in the 1980s and 1990s. The recent recovery of production has not been accompanied by significant improvements in the well being of all its citizens. Infant mortality remains unacceptably high at 92 per 1,000 births in 1992. Life expectancy at birth is only 51 years, very little changed over the past two decades. Primary school enrolment has fallen from

93 per cent in 1980 to less than 69 per cent in 1990, and the secondary school gross enrolment rate is only 4 per cent compared with the sub-Saharan African average of 17 per cent. After almost 35 years of independence and significant external assistance, most Tanzanians, as well as donors, expected more. Improving the welfare of the poor and strengthening programmes in education and health are now matters of expressed priority, but action still lags behind words.

At the same time as it has been engaged in economic reforms, Tanzania has also been undertaking major adjustment in its political system. The country is now in the midst of its first multi-party parliamentary and presidential election campaign, reported on by a vigorous and outspoken range of independent newspapers that have emerged over the past few years of political liberalisation. The dual transition – in the economic and political systems – is obviously highly challenging to the government. Wherever it has been attempted elsewhere in the world, it has proved tricky to navigate.

1.3 Difficult Transitions/Changing Needs

The government of Tanzania's programmes for macroeconomic stabilisation and structural adjustment initially featured significant exchange-rate devaluation and tightened fiscal discipline. The main elements of such short- to medium-term stabilisation measures could be managed effectively by a relatively small number of political leaders and technocrats from the central economic ministries and institutions and, as has been seen, the Tanzanian record in this respect, until recently, has been relatively good.

The longer-term transition from socialist to market institutions is more far-reaching and must involve far more actors, both within the government and in the broader economy, than the implementation of stabilisation measures. Such deeper structural and institutional change is therefore considerably more demanding, both in terms of public understanding and support and in expertise. As the experience in many other countries has shown, the dismantling of the state and the encouragement of market entrants involve the creation of a whole new 'culture' and a wholly new role for government. It has typically been easier and faster to eliminate the previous governmental rules and institutions than to institute new ones appropriate to the emerging market economy. The new role of government in a market economy is narrower and more focused upon 'core activities', but it is no less demanding of skill and integrity in the public service. The so-called 'second generation' reforms typically take more time and more care; they are unlikely to prove fruitful if they are unduly rushed. Moreover, the replacement of the old behavioral norms and institutions with the 'freedom' of the market inevitably, for a time, generates a degree of chaos and unrestrained pursuit of personal gain and private capital accumulation.

As noted above, these major changes in economic organisation are accompanied in Tanzania, as in many other countries, by a major political transition. Political liberalisation involves increased formal transparency and accountability in the government, and increased public debate with regard to policy directions. It also requires the elaboration of new and detailed procedures for public decision-making, accountability and monitoring, and the gradual build-up of experience and precedents within the new political system. The political reforms may therefore have the side effect of further slowing some elements of economic policy reform and institutional change about which many donors feel the GoT has already been slow enough. At the same time, the newly free press tends (properly) to highlight corruption, inefficiency, high-level disagreements and other less attractive features of the transitional economic order and, in its less responsible quarters, may exaggerate them.

Ironically, progress in the transparency of governmental activities has contributed to the sense among donors and many Tanzanians that the government is not functioning well. The detailed figures attesting to the existence of illegalities in the tax system and the likelihood of attendant corruption, which have only recently become available, are themselves the product of reforms in the Tanzanian control and disclosure system. Although corruption is probably equally common in many other countries, and may have been just as common in Tanzania itself in an earlier period, it was the release of these figures in November 1994 that brought the crisis in the aid relationship in Tanzania to a head[2].

---

[2] Subsequent detailed analysis of the tax losses announced in November have revealed that of the Tsh. 70 bn 'lost', Tsh. 50 bn were the product of legal exemptions, some of which could, of course , have been granted for improper reasons; of the remaining Tsh. 20 bn, only Tsh. 5 bn were hardcore tax arrears, Tsh. 2.5 bn of which have already been collected. Some Tanzanians and donor observers now feel that the initial reactions to the figures, on the part of both the government and the donors, may have been exaggerated. The underlying concerns over revenue losses and/or corruption nevertheless remain universal.

2. THE QUESTION OF 'OWNERSHIP'
2.1 The Ownership Situation

In contemporary debates about aid policy there is much discussion of the importance of 'ownership'. Both the Development Assistance Committee of the OECD, in its statement of 'principles for effective aid', and the World Bank, in a variety of studies and statements, acknowledge the importance of national 'ownership' of development projects and programmes, however great their external inputs. This importance is widely seen to derive not only from its inherent appropriateness but also from its efficacy. Projects and programmes that are locally owned, at least by those who have to implement them have proved more likely to work and to be sustained.

In our consultations many people, both donors and Tanzanians, alleged weak Tanzanian ownership of the programmes and projects for which aid is received. We found, however, that, like many such modish expressions, the word 'ownership' is loosely used and rarely defined. Some usages seem decidedly eccentric, as with the statement from one aid agency that 'we have pressured the GoT to accept ownership of ...' Another stated, 'we want them to take ownership. Of course, they must do what we want. If not, they should get their money elsewhere'.

Various indicators can be used to establish the ownership of a programme or project. Whose objectives does it reflect, the recipient government's or the donors'? Who initiated, designed and evaluated it? To what extent do leading members of the government support controversial policies and programmes in public speeches, and how vigorous is the government in 'selling' them to the wider public? To what extent has the public been consulted in the preparatory stages of a project/programme in order to achieve a consensus, and to what extent has responsibility for it been developed upon those it most affects? In negative terms, local ownership may be indicated by the relative absence of donor conditionality, just as heavy conditionality is a sure sign of weak national ownership. But even when the answers to these questions indicate that donor ownership is initially dominant, there is still the possibility that ownership may be transferred to the government during implementation.

Local ownership is thus at its greatest where aided activities reflect local goals and priorities, preferably based on a genuinely consultative national consensus, where the identification of projects and programmes to be assisted rests primarily with the recipient government and where there is minimal resort by donors to policy conditionality (as distinct from the standard stipulations concerning accounting, procurement, etc.). None of this, of course, precludes extensive and early-stage consultation with donor agencies in order to arrive at outcomes which satisfy the objectives of all parties (as Tanzania's Planning Commission has done in the preparation of its Rolling Plan and Forward Budget). Nevertheless, ownership must mean that the final decisions rest with the recipient government.

We concur in the view that, despite some admirable exceptions to which we shall refer again, the ownership situation in Tanzania is at present unsatisfactory. The exceptions include, most notably, the Integrated Roads Programme, which was presented to us as a case of transferred ownership, with first phase largely donor-driven but the second phase (after a tug–of–war with donors) largely designed and administered by Tanzanians. Many interviewees noted that it may be difficult to apply this 'transfer' model to programmes which are more complex and have wider social ramifications. In any event, such transitional devices are second best to programmes which start life as well-prepared government initiatives. Although we were given conflicting views on this, it appears that there may be signs of ownership transfer beginning in the recently developed social sector strategy – initially a creature of the World Bank but now espoused with some enthusiasm by departments of the GoT. (A larger problem, in this case, appears to be poor consultation with other interested donors, see section 4 of this report).

In other areas, however, it is clear that the situation is poor. The case of civil service reform was mentioned several times as a donor-driven process for which, while there was a good deal of support within the civil service, there was little or no backing at the political level. In this case weak leadership is holding back the improvement of public administration. Technical cooperation was another area in which local ownership appeared typically weak. Notwithstanding donor agreement in the OECD to a set of principles which includes 'greater emphasis on the central role of developing countries in the planning, design and management of technical cooperations', the reality is that much of the technical assistance is involuntary, with many TC personnel present in the country only at donor insistence. A recent UNDP-commissioned study of technical assistance found that:

In almost all African Countries.... aid donors orchestrate the technical cooperation show. They conceive most project ideas, arrange their design, hire most of the experts, and oversee implementation ... This situation has many costs and inconveniences. The most general and significant is that African authorities feel little ownership of activities with which they have been so little involved, making commitment problematic... Almost everybody agrees about the basic remedy for these problems: much greater responsibility for management of technical cooperation has to be transferred to local hands.

(Elliot J. Berg (Coordinator), Rethinking Technical Cooperation, New York: UNDP and Development Alternative Inc., 1993; pp. 249 – 50).

On the basis of our necessarily somewhat superficial overview, we see the experience of technical cooperation in Tanzania as fully consistent with these wider findings.

Even when there is genuine donor-GoT agreement as to general policy on some particular subject, we heard numerous and varied complaints that this did not prevent intrusive donor conditionality at the level of detailed implementation. Bilateral donors were mentioned as having their own individual agendas, being reluctant to conform to GoT priorities (on the occasions when these were expressed), and paying little more than lip service to the principle of local ownership. This was stressed, for example, by the Ministry of Education, which found itself overwhelmed by the specific conditionalities of a multitude of donors; and there were many others.

Although it appears that the October 1994 Policy Framework Paper (PFP) was a collaborative effort, in the preparation of which the GoT was engaged and which reasonably reflected its own policies, two related complaints were made about the operation of the PFP process. First, although there had reportedly been a reasonable amount of give and take between the GoT and the IMF World Bank in finalising the paper (an improvement on earlier negotiations), the original draft was in fact prepared in Washington. The GoT therefore found itself negotiating amendments to a document prepared by others, thus producing an outcome which doubtless differed substantially from that which would have resulted from a more genuinely consensus-building process. Second, after it was agreed, the World Bank then effectively reneged on the PFO by introducing new conditionalities during the negotiating of a new structural adjustment credit (because, we were told, there had been a turnover in key Bank personnel and the Bank had decided the PFP was inadequate).

> **RECOMMENDATION 2:** *The GoT should insist on its right to prepare the first drafts of future PFPs, Letters of Intent and Letters of Development Policy, and the IFIs should honour that right. The final versions of these documents must, of course, be jointly agreed and this places a requirement on the government to be realistic in its approaches to these tasks.*

Looking at the ownership situation more widely, our impression is that the case of civil service reform was typical of a wide range of other policy areas. Many initiatives originate with donors, with only limited policy guidance from the GoT – weaknesses often exacerbated by the limited capacity of the civil service to initiate and manage programmes and projects. Senior members of the government complained to us about the diminishing capabilities of the public administration, a lament echoed by several donors. We were told, for example, that the German aid officials had found it impossible to adhere to their country's policy of working through local administrations because many District administrations were barely functioning.

> **RECOMMENDATION 3:** *The capabilities of the public administration at all levels need to be enhanced. This seems to be widely recognised and donors are anxious to help. However, here too the GoT should ensure that it remains in charge and should strongly resist the imposition of technical assistance which has been common hitherto.*

We will return to these matters in Section 4.

2.2 Source of Weakness

How has such an unsatisfactory situation come about? Both donors and the GoT have contributed to it. Various donor practices undermine the possibilities of local ownership. Most major donors prepare medium-term country strategies or programmes, to which their specific project and technical cooperation decisions can be related, and which reflect the overall priorities of their aid policies. It is entirely proper that donors should develop their own aid policies and it is desirable that these should have at least a medium-term time horizon. Moreover, as a practical matter, it is probably inevitable that these exercises should reflect the imperatives of donor parliamentary and administrative timetables. However, there is a considerable tension between donors' desire to have their own country aid strategies and their stated wish that there should be local ownership. Reconciliation of these two objectives would require country programmes to be worked out collaboratively and iteratively (similar to the manner in which PFPs are supposed to be prepared).

In varying degrees, donor's practices fall short of this ideal. While some (for example, Denmark and Norway) do enter into such consultations, others appear to view the matter as one for their autonomous decision-making. Thus, a recent evaluation of Dutch aid to Tanzania notes that:

Since 1985, three country policy documents for Tanzania have been produced, namely, for the periods 1985–1988; 1989–1992; and 1992–1995. They are prepared (by the aid agency) and the recipient countries are not involved in their preparation. The documents thus serve mainly as a framework for planning and programming on the donor side... (Despite improvements), country programme planning, however remains a strongly donor-driven process. The policy consultations hardly leave room for a dialogue about policy options and priorities in the development cooperation programme.

(Evaluation of the Netherlands Development Programme with Tanzania, 1970 – 1992, Operation Review Unit, Ministry of Foreign Affairs, 1994, pp. 102-03).

The Dutch Embassy in Dar es Salaam is currently preparing a new strategy paper, which clearly will be characterised by a similar lack of consultation. While we have not been able to explore their details, it is our impression that the procedures of a number of other donors have similar defects. It goes without saying that these undermine GoT ownership of aided programmes and projects.

Donor practices undermine ownership in other ways too. We were given a number of instances, for example in the area of primary education, where agencies manipulate their choices of government departments to work with, and their entry points into them, in order to achieve their own objectives. We were also told of instances when, faced with government reluctance to agree to a donor's project, the ambassador would implicitly threaten that the general level of his country's support might be scaled down. It also appears to be quite a common practice (welcomed, no doubt, by the

Tanzanian beneficiaries) for donors to co-opt, or to pay 'incentives' to GoT officials working on their projects. As one respondent pointed out, where this is extensive it comes close to turning government departments into provider of private consultancy services, seriously undermining the GoT's capabilities for exercising ownership.

The forces pushing bilateral donor agencies in directions which undermine GoT ownership are varied and deep-seated. Each donor has its own aid policies and 'agenda', and is anxious to pursue its own objectives even when these are not shared by the government. Constitutional, parliamentary and accounting requirements, aimed at ensuring proper accountability for the use of taxpayers' money, may also increase donor intrusiveness, a tendency that can only be enhanced by the perception already noted that corruption is a large and growing problem in Tanzania. It is also likely that agency staff will be under pressure to ensure that they spend their budgets, even if it requires a degree of bulldozing to achieve this result, and they may well see it as in their own career interests to secure a high level of aid giving or lending. They are also under pressure to show quick results and short-term efficiency. There are few rewards for those who are prepared to sacrifice short-term performance for the sake of slower but more sustainable progress.

We have also observed that it is relatively rare for donor agencies to delegate substantial responsibilities to their field offices. Most are fairly centralised in structure, regarding their local offices largely as implementation agencies with little autonomous spending or other powers. Yet it is the local offices which, by dint of their everyday exposure to local realities and government officials, best understand local aspirations and constraints.

RECOMMENDATION 4: *Substantial changes are needed in the operational culture of bilateral donors. Above all, they need to take far more seriously at the country level the general principles and support for local ownership espoused by policymakers in their headquarters. The gap between rhetoric and reality must be narrowed and donors must cease practices which undermine the exercise of Treasury control and other normal operations of the public administration. A greater willingness to devolve responsibilities to local offices would make it easier to harmonise donor and GoT interests.*

Then there is the World Bank. We have no wish to single out any particular agency, but the range of criticisms we heard of the Bank on this subject was too extensive to be ignored and our discussions at the Bank's resident mission were not reassuring. While there was widespread appreciation of the Bank's efforts to disseminate information on its activities, there was virtual unanimity among other donors that it was unwilling to engage in serious substantive discussions. As one bilateral donor official put it to us, 'there is no way that the Bank can be influenced in what it has made up its mind to do'. The perception is of an institution encouraged by its superior manpower and other resources to be self-confident to the point of arrogance, with little consideration of others' views. Local ownership is the first casualty of such an attitude, as illustrated by the fact, reported to us, that in the preparation of technical cooperation projects, the Bank staff routinely drafts terms of reference, instead of leaving that to GoT (The Bank is not alone in this practice). In the words of a Bank official, 'I know that's not ideal but it's the only way to do business here.'

On the donor side, we can sum up by reporting that we found a vast lack of contact between the general principles to which donor headquarters pay lip service and the reality in the field. We have already contrasted the DAC principles on technical cooperation with the involuntary nature (from the Tanzanian standpoint) of much of this activity in Tanzania. (Technical cooperation makes up about 20 per cent of estimated net ODA to Tanzania from all sources). There is an equally striking difference between the remark just quoted about 'doing business' in Tanzania and the well-known criticisms by the World Bank's Vice President responsible for Africa of the adverse effects on government capabilities of over-reliance on foreign experts and donor neglect of the importance of local ownership. In practice, the Bank (along with other donors) ignores the first conclusion of its own recent report on aid effectiveness, that 'aid is most effective when it supports programmes and projects that are "owned" by the recipient country' (Development Issues, no. 34, Presentation to the 49 the Meeting of the Development Committee, Madrid, 3 October 1994, p. 27).

RECOMMENDATION 5: *(a) Taking ownership seriously entails donor willingness to withhold or delay aid until the local conditions necessary for ownership are satisfied; a*

culture which is willing to override ownership in order to
'do business' is inconsistent with all that has been learned
about how aid can be made more effective; a longer-term
time horizon is needed than some of the donors display, for
all their long past association with country.

(b) Taking ownership seriously also entails that donor's
country strategies should blend both with the donors' policies
and those of the GoT through a process of iteration, and
that consultation on these should begin at an early stage.

(c) Our recommendations on donor culture apply with
particular force to the World Bank.

Turning now to the government side of the equation, we are bound to be critical here too. Several donors and some people from the GoT commented on the passivity of the government in the face of multiple donors, its apparent lack of ambition to impose its will and priorities on them and its reluctance to say 'no'. The GoT doubtless feels too greatly in need of the assistance to be able to take a strong position, but various donors contrasted its rather supine attitude with countries ostensibly in no less need of aid. The governments of Eritrea and Ethiopia were particularly mentioned in this context. Refusal of offers of assistance which do not fit in with agreed priorities may appear risky to the GoT; but we believe that the superficially high risk of such a stance is largely illusory, since experience has shown that inappropriate, donor-driven aid brings few lasting benefits. The GoT appears to suffer from an 'aid-dependence syndrome', which has created an attitude of mind in which, over time, it comes to be expected that most initiatives will originate from the donors, while the government and its officials feel overwhelmed by the magnitude of the task of trying to impose their own will. Our belief is that, if it were minded to do so, the government could impose much more authority on the donors than it does at present. We also believe that the donors, although somewhat ambivalent on this, would come to accept it, as they have done elsewhere.

Such action would require strong political leadership and a clear consensus on the desirable direction for the country and on its priorities – in other words, a vision for the future. However, it was widely commented to us from all sides that at present the government lacks vision. It is to be hoped that the government which emerges after the pending elections will be able to provide more leadership of this kind and to restore greater discipline to the aid scene. We return to these matters in the following sections.

RECOMMENDATION 6: *In consultation with the wider public, civil society and the donor community, the incoming GoT should urgently formulate a clear, practical, medium – to long-term development strategy for the country and be far more vigorous in seeking to impose the resulting policy and project priorities on the donors.*

3. DONOR COORDINATION AND AID EFFECTIVENESS

The DAC principles on aid effectiveness identify two major propositions with regard to effective aid coordination. First, both recipients and donors should adhere to carefully appraised and productive investment programmes, in line with consultatively established priorities, as the basis for allocating aid and monitoring implementation. Secondly, the DAC principles emphasise that full and frank exchanges of information on ongoing and planned activities among donors, and between donors and recipients, are essential to the successful coordination and effective use of aid (OECD, DAC Principles for Effective Aid, Paris: OECD, 1992, p.25). In our interviews with different interested parties in and outside Tanzania we found strong agreement with these principles.

Preliminary work has begun towards the preparation of a 'core' investment programme as a guide both to aid allocation and to the subsequent monitoring of implementation. The Rolling Plan and Forward Budget currently under preparation by the Planning Commission is being supplemented by sectoral strategies for the social services sector, agriculture, infrastructure and the civil service. A modest start has also been made towards the proposed exchange of start information. Such exchanges now take place at the DAC donors meetings on the first Thursday of every month, the Joint Government – Donor meetings held once a month, and the Joint Evaluation Committee and Joint Management Committee monthly meetings.

3.1 Concerns about Aid Coordination

The problems with regard to aid effectiveness and coordination in Tanzania remain, at their roots, the result of failure to match individual donor and government agencies' interests with agreed and coordinate priorities. Operationally, the situation is characterised by uncoordinated proliferation of projects across a large number of donors and a wide variety of disbursement accounting arrangements. In our interviews with donors and the government of Tanzania alike, reference was often made to the more than 2,000 projects and the 40 donors that have been involved in aid to Tanzania. We also heard that weak coordination capacity and lack of authority on the part of the GoT were making overall coordination among donors extremely difficult. Donor-driven proliferation of projects was to a large extent, a reflection of this weakness as well as the product of strong donor vested interests in their own identifiable 'monuments'.

There is much more lip service to coordination, it seems to us, than there is commitment and action. Time and again we heard from all concerned of the need to reduce the number of projects and to adopt a sectoral focus or concentration. Similarly, many people emphasised the importance of harmonising country programmes with Tanzania's own prioritisation of projects. Yet effective prioritisation on the part of the GoT has still to be developed, and donors' willingness to abide by it remains, on the evidence, mixed at best. In the absence of such prioritisation and the political will to respect it on all sides, frustrations will persist.

Concern was frequently expressed about the recent trend on the part of donors towards setting up parallel project management systems in order to circumvent the problem of weak GoT capacity. This is correctly seen as worsening the already serious problems crated by project proliferation. There has been increasing recognition that such practices discourage the development of coherent and integrated management systems and weaken the incentives for coordination.

RECOMMENDATION 7: *The GoT should take steps, in collaboration with donors, to achieve common arrangements for project implementation and to avoid the recent proliferation of parallel project management systems. Increased effort should be exerted to develop Tanzanian capacity for management at all levels of programme and project implementation.*

Another new development, of concern particularly to the GoT, is the proliferation of entry points for donors. These now include local governments, local communities and other NGOs. These entities offer donors the advantages of flexibility, closeness to target

20

populations and potential for rapid intervention unencumbered by government bureaucracy. However, the strengthening of these channels may be at the expense of the adherence to overall investment priorities of policy guidelines. Of even more concern to many people is the apparent willingness on the part of some donors to consider this as a substitute for strengthening government capacity. Such approaches run the risk of creating NGOs that are simply the clients of particular donors. Better coordination could be achieved among those working with these new partners if there were appropriate consultation with public authorities.

RECOMMENDATION 8: *There is an immediate need to harmonise procedures and provide information as to appropriate donor entry points for project support in order to ensure that the coordination and policy roles of public authorities are preserved. This can be done without prejudice to the strong advantages of utilising more decentralised channels of assistance.*

Lack of coordination among GoT agencies was another problem we heard about from both donors and the GoT. Most people agree that the Planning Commission and the Treasury ought to play lead roles in fostering coordination. As the situation now stands, sectoral ministries de facto negotiate their own projects which are subsequently registered by these higher authorities without clear guidelines or priorities as to investment or policy. Those we interviewed in the GoT see this problem as the product partly of weakness in political leadership and partly of weakness in the capacities of core ministries to provide adequate guidance. Much of the Planning Commission's activity, for example, has been directed to inherently peripheral undertakings such as the facilitation of workshops, studies and consultations rather than to its main function, the provision of direction for the economy.

The need to develop a vision for long-term development and to draw up supportive strategies and investment programmes was often expressed by interviewees, and was widely seen as essential for determining overall priorities and avoiding the omission of important activities. An overall strategy should be the basis for developing rolling plans for implementation and should serve as the guide for sectoral programmes. The sectoral ministries, in this general view, should in turn use the agreed priorities as the basis for the details of their own sectoral strategies and project master plans. To complement these measures it was suggested that a clear delineation of functions should be provided and that public expenditure review systems for monitoring and planning should be strengthened.

We also heard frequently of the need to coordinate individual donor country programmes with the investment priorities developed by the GoT. Reference was often made to the critical role of donor field offices in this regard, since they are best placed to advise on harmonising donor and recipient interests. Preparations for the annual bilateral donor consultation meetings are a critical part of the process of such harmonisation and should ensure that individual donor headquarters are in tune with relevant developments in investment programming and prioritisation in Tanzania.

RECOMMENDATION 9: *The process of arriving at the core priorities should be consultative in order to facilitate compliance at the implementation stage. In this regard it is necessary that there is harmonisation between individual donor country programmes and the agreed prioritisation. Both the Planning Commission and the Treasury should assume leading roles in ensuring this harmonisation through their annual bilateral consultations with donors.*

Finally we heard about the need for full disclosure of committed donor resources for the purposes of proper budgetary planning. A significant part of development expenditures is not channeled through the GoT. This problem relates in particular to expenditures incurred outside Tanzania or made directly by donors, particularly for technical cooperation and project assistance in the form of commodities. Such 'Direct Funds' remain, for the most part, unrecorded in the Tanzanian Development budget. Although the GoT has asked for this information ex ante, only one donor so far has agreed to provide it.

RECOMMENDATION 10: *To the extent that public expenditure review systems become the fulcrum of planning and monitoring, it is imperative that the GoT should seek and obtain full information on resource commitments both from within and from outside the country. Even if the exact amounts of Direct Funds may not be available, some estimates could be provided to allow them to be taken into account in programmatic planning.*

3.2 Current Arrangements for Aid Coordination

There are useful lessons to be learned from the contrast between the relative success of coordination in the balance-of-payment (BOP) support for macroeconomic reforms and structural adjustment, on the one hand, and the fragmented support for development projects on the other.

The IMF and the World Bank have played lead roles in coordinating programme support for Tanzania. The IMF has coordinated overall BOP support though its stipulation of programme benchmarks and schedules for implementation. The GoT's involvement in this process is via the Inter-Ministerial Technical Committee (IMTC) whose task is to negotiate and review the content and implementation schedule for policy reforms included in the Policy Framework Paper or other agreements with the IMF. These detailed agreements are the main instruments for determining the actual content of the reform programme over a specific period and for monitoring performance.

Other donors co-finance BOP support based on the Fund's assessment as to whether or not programme implementation is on track. Joint local monitoring instruments have been set up to review performance on a monthly basis. The monthly Joint Evaluation Committee meetings co-chaired by the Treasury and the Bank of Tanzania serve as the main local monitoring device.

The World Bank, for its part, plays a lead role in the coordination of sectoral support. This role is based on its (IDA) sectoral lending programmes, offered in various phases under the general rubric of its Structural Adjustment Programmes. Benchmarks for implementation are included in the PFP to serve both as action plans and as monitoring instruments. Co-financing by other donors is triggered by the World Bank's assessment of performance. Sectoral ministries are involved via the IMTC in negotiating the framework for support and subsequent reviews of implementation. The monthly Joint Government-Donor Meeting is the key local monitoring device in this regard, with Joint Evaluation Committee meetings reviewing benchmarks and monitoring performance on an ongoing basis.

Under both types of programme lending bilateral donors have been highly dependent on the two multilateral financial institutions for assessments of performance. This passive stance is changing, however, with respect to sectoral programmes, as evidenced by the bilateral donors' increased calls for more active involvement in the design of social sector strategy and civil service reforms, in both of which their experience in the country is highly significant. Such a change requires increased consultations with the GoT, which must now be expected to play a more effective lead role; all sides are, in principle, agreed on this.

Development project support, on the other hand, continues to lack coordination. Unfortunately, this is the area in which donor assistance has been most dominant and where proliferation of projects and modalities for support is most prevalent. Many of the concerns raised earlier relate to this large segment of aid in Tanzania.

The GoT has begun to rationalise the large portfolio of public investment projects financed through its development budget. As already noted, a core investment programme was identified for the first time in 1993/94 as part of the Rolling Plan and Forward Budget, with the GoT committing up to 80 percent of its own development budget resource to this core. It is planned to increase this share to 90 per cent. Projects identified under the 'Super Core' are to receive 100 per cent of funding requirements. The GoT is calling on donors to cooperate in this nascent process of rationalising the development budget. (Related issues are discussed below in Section 4 of this report).

Similarly, at the sectoral level, the current effort is to develop sectoral strategies with related sub sectoral 'Project Master Plans' to guide resource commitments both from within and from outside the country. The considerable success of the Integrated Roads Programme in coordinating support in this way under a well-developed strategy has received wide acknowledgement. Developments with regard to the social sector strategy, agricultural sector policy and the civil service reform programme are all aimed at emulating this success. Sub sectoral programmes in Education and Health are also on the drawing board, albeit at very preliminary stages. What is important to note is that these undertakings all involve the GoT and donors in consultative processes.

In view of the strong vested interests on the part of both ministries and donors in maintaining established project portfolios, the challenges in making the transition from the existing situation of an uncoordinated proliferation of projects to a more rationalised and focused programme are formidable. Realism requires that some short –term flexibility be allowed in order to avoid excessive waste from a sudden truncation of ongoing projects and to enable a smooth transition to take place. Transitional 'space' is also needed to accommodate legal changes in country programmes on the donors' side. Transitional measures should include an orderly phasing out of existing non-priority projects and the confinement of new commitments to those projects identified in the core investment programme. It is imperative, however, that all parties concerned should be resolute and should embark on the necessary changes as soon as possible.

RECOMMENDATION 11: *The central coordinating role in all development endeavours ought to be that of the GoT. Two key instruments are essential in this regard: (i) a clearly articulated investment programme identifying priorities based on an overall development strategy, which is in turn converted into Rolling Plan and Forward Budget as currently being developed; (ii) a public expenditure review system which should serve both as the basis for resource allocation and as an instrument for monitoring implementation. The implications for recurrent costs of the provisions of the investment programme must also be taken into account within such a comprehensive review system.*
We can not overemphasise the need to foster strong political commitment among the GoT and donors in adhering to the agreed prioritisation in project support, including subjecting bilateral negotiations and the drawing up of country programmes to these priorities.

The above endeavours still lack appropriate mechanisms for implementation and coordination between the overall investment programme and individual sectoral strategies. A clear functional structure for decisions, guidance, and implementation needs to be developed and adhered to. The strengthening of civil service capacity more generally and of the core ministries in particular is fundamental to the successful implementation of the above arrangements.

RECOMMENDATION 12: *To the extent possible, donor support should be organised sector-wide or within subsectoral project master plans developed under each ministry. In this way individual donor interventions can be harmonised along the lines of common policies and strategies. Arrangements need to be in place to allow coordination across all donors involved in a specific sector. Therefore, in addition to the* *more general fora for exchange of information, sectoral ministries should organise specific coordinating meetings to discuss prospective programmes and review implementation, and donors should formally commit themselves to work through them.*

3.3 Further Dimensions of Coordination and Aid Effectiveness

In only a few cases do individual donor countries coordinate the assistance they provide in the form of new aid flows with what they offer in the form of debt relief. This is apparent at the global level in the separate meetings held by the Consultative Group, which essentially focuses on new commitments, and the Paris Club, which focuses on debt relief. In these two fora, both held in Paris, the main donor agencies involved are distinct, and negotiations on the two types of assistance are thus separate. Depending on how much coordination there is between treasury and Development Cooperation agencies in each donor country, disjunction in information may occur. We recognise the fact that the CG meetings consider the financing requirements inclusive of debt relief, but the difference in the timing of the two meetings makes it difficult to obtain complete information when required.

For many years, analysts of official bilateral debt have urged greater coordination between the Paris Club and aid donor meetings such as the Consultative Groups and Round Tables (RT). Comparing the two, the CGs and RTs have the distinct advantage in that they set the overall framework for external assistance. The Paris Club must take this framework into account in its decisions if an integrated treatment of financing needs is to be achieved. Such coordination would permit a closer monitoring of the additionality of debt relief measures, which since 1988 have involved increasing concessionality, in the meeting of financing requirements. Moreover, if the coordination could be done by merging the two sets of meetings, it would greatly reduce the current high 'transactions' costs which are an excessively heavy burden on the scarce financial and managerial resources of countries such as Tanzania. These transaction costs derive from the intensive inputs of time, energy and travel that go into the preparation, negotiations and monitoring of the outcomes from the two separate sets of meetings. Initial steps towards their merger could include the introduction of cross-references in the agenda and each set of meetings to decisions made in the other.

RECOMMENDATION 13: *Individual donor countries, through prior consultation among the relevant agencies, should combine their assistance given in the forms of new commitments and of debt relief so as to provide a basis for accurate and timely determination of financing requirements. This should also assist in determining the complete net resource envelope for budgeting purposes. First steps should be taken towards the reduction of transactions costs via the consolidation of CG and Paris Club meetings. The Tanzania case is among the most obviously deserving of such innovation.*

Stability of the joint development effort is also important for the future of a reformed relationship between the GoT and its aid donors. Without confidence that new GoT policies and programmes will be sustained, economic decision-makers in Tanzania, both private and public, may be restrained in their responses to them and thus in their contributions to Tanzanian development. In Tanzania, as elsewhere, the credibility of government policies and programmes is fundamentally important to the decisions of private savers and investors. Development programmes like those of the GoT are inevitably vulnerable to adverse and unpredictable shocks from the terms of trade, the weather or capita flows. Every effort should be made to maintain the continuity and credibility of Tanzanian development programmes by making provisions, in advance, to reduce the impact of adverse shocks through the provision of offsetting non-project finance.

RECOMMENDATION 14: *To increase the credibility of the GoT's longer-term strategies and plans, efforts will be required to stabilise government revenues and development expenditures. Donors should support such efforts, to the degree that their own rules permit, with longer–term commitments and contingency financing arrangements to protect Tanzanian programmes against unexpected adverse shocks.*

4. RESPONSIBILITIES OF THE GOVERNMENT OF TANZANIA

Many of the key responsibilities devolving on the GoT, in connection with efforts on the part of all parties to restore good aid relationships, have already been discussed. In this section, we shall repeat some of them – and add some more.

Both to improve effective utilisation of foreign aid and to mobilise and utilise domestic resources efficiently to promote poverty alleviating growth, Tanzania's national leadership needs to articulate a development vision – a vision that inspires its own population and provides hope for the future. A broad-based development vision is bound to include objectives that are not new to Tanzania's development philosophy: commitment to universal and relevant primary education, access to basic primary health care, clean water for all, local community participation, and broad –based agricultural and rural development. A clear commitment in words and deeds to regulatory framework that is supportive to the private sector in general and rural households in particular is also required. The main building blocks of Tanzania's development vision are already implicit in government statements, but they have not been articulated coherently. More important, as has been seen, there is a widespread perception, not only among donors but also among the general Tanzanian public, that the national leadership does not have a coherent development programme of its own, about which it is enthusiastic or even passionate, but is simply responding to proposals from aid donors, the World Bank and the IMF. As one major donor put it to us, 'They seem tired. That fight of earlier years is gone, absolutely gone'.

Articulation of a development vision is inadequate without the design of sound policies and the building of an effective administrative and institutional structure capable of implementing and reviewing development policies and communicating with and learning from those affected by these policies. Promoting broad-based development requires a recognition of the resource constraints facing the government, and the mobilisation and allocation of financial resources in the priority sectors. To donors that are interested in supporting poverty alleviation and broad – based development, government effort in revenue collection and expenditure allocations to sectors that increase the capabilities of the poor are barometers of the government's commitment to the promotion of development.

There is a general consensus among donors, senior government officials and well-informed members of the public that the government machinery is at present very weak. Formulation and implementation of government economic policy, and overall economic management, are undoubtedly in disarray.

The current weakness of the public administration has a long history. Among its causes were the numerous institutional and administrative changes considered necessary to promote rapid socialist development in the 1960's and the 1970's. With the benefit of hindsight, it can be seen that measures undertaken by the government – including extensive nationalisation of commercial enterprises; decentralisation of central government and the removal of local governments; villagisation; abolition of cooperatives and the introduction of the multi-purpose crop authorities; expansion of the party bureaucracy under the auspices of a supreme single-party system; intensive politicisation of the civil service and employees of public enterprises; and popularisation of workers' control and participation in management — overextended the role of government beyond its administrative capacity and resource availability, while at the same time undermining discipline, the work ethic and the link between responsibility and accountability. The rapid fall in the purchasing power of wages and salaries and the development of parallel markets at the beginning of the 1980s further eroded the morale and morality of the civil service, contributing to the increasing inefficiency of the government in the delivery of public services.

4.1 Civil Service Reform

The improvement of government performance is to be pursued by implementing a civil service reform that aims at having 'a smaller, affordable, well-compensated, efficient and effectively performing civil service working to implement redefined policies and strategies for national economic development and delivery of public services... The specific objectives of this programme are:

(a) to redefine the roles and functions of the government with a view to hiving-off functions not considered to be relevant, reducing the scope of government operations to an affordable scale, and restructuring its organisation and operations to achieve efficiency and effectiveness in the delivery of public services;

(b) to control the size and growth of government employment so that overmanning is eliminated and the government can ultimately afford to competitively compensate its employees;

(c) to improve the quality, capacity, productivity and performance of the civil servants through improvements in the systems and procedures for personnel recruitment, deployment, grading and promotions, training and discipline;

(d) to rationalise and enhance civil service pay by eliminating the distortions and anomalies that have crept into the system, and by improving total compensation at all levels so that it meets the minimum household living requirements and is commensurate with the qualifications, skills experience and responsibilities of individual civil servants; and

(e) to support the decentralisation of government functions by rationalising central and local government linkages, and facilitating further transfer of authority, responsibilities and resources to the regions and districts'. (Civil Service Reform Programme)

To manage the programme and mobilise its funding, the civil service reform has been dis-aggregated into the following six components:

- retrenchment and redeployment;
- personnel control and management;
- pay reform;
- organisation and efficiency reviews;
- capacity building and training; and
- local government reforms.

The main problem facing the reform, and one which is likely to undermine its implementation, is the fact that it appears to lack 'political ownership' at the national level. It is largely seen as a programme of retrenchment with the possibility of 'golden handshakes' rather than as a programme of increased efficiency to deliver better public services.

By the end of the 1994/95 fiscal year, the government expects to fulfill the PFP requirement of retrenching 50,000 civil servants (including the removal of ghost workers); most of the retrenched workers have received some compensation. Net budgetary savings from retrenchment have unfortunately not been as great as might be expected. Those who are retrenched are typically low-salaried workers who do not receive the large allowance which are, in fact, more important in overall remuneration. The share of wages and salaries in total government expenditure is , in any case, only about 25 per cent.

The 1994 Public Expenditure Review (PER), which was prepared under the leadership of the World Bank, nevertheless suggested that:

To complete the retrenchment exercise within a reasonable time frame, the government should revise its targets upwards to retrench at least 40,000 instead of 20,000 civil servants on a net basis per year for the next three years. (p. v)

So far the civil service reform, focusing on retrenchment and compensation of retrenchees, has neither saved significant sums nor laid the foundation for improving the efficiency of the civil service. Similar approaches are unlikely to do better in the future. The efficiency of government ministries is expected to be improved, however, by implementing the recommendations from the organisation and efficiency reviews which aim to streamline the government structure.

The Secretariat of the Civil Service Reform Commission has completed four such reviews – for the Ministry of Finance, the Civil Service Department, the Planning Commission and the Prime Minister's Office. It is also in the process of completing reviews for the Ministries of Health; Education; and Science, Technology and Higher Education. There is as yet, however, no clear system for ensuring response or implementation of the Secretariat's recommendations. For example, by mid April 1995 the Secretariat had received no response from the Planning Commission and the Prime Minister's Office to the recommendations it had submitted in December 1994. The absence of a quick response to the Commission's proposals is surprising, given that the Steering Committee of the Civil Service Reform is composed of the Principal Secretaries of the Prime Minister's Office, the Planning Commission, the Treasury, and the Labour and Civil Service Departments. Moreover, the task force which conducted the organisation and efficiency reviews consists of the Deputy Principal Secretaries of the Treasury, the President's Office, the Prime Minister's Office, and the Planning Commission, and the Director of Management and Services of the Civil Service Department. Given the participation of senior officials from the central ministries in both the Steering Committee and the task force, their recommendations and to organisation of the four ministries with which they began should already be familiar.

Without the national leadership providing the general guidelines and taking the political responsibility for the difficult decisions required, the civil service reform may end up being an exercise in little more than producing reports. Delay during the election period is understandable. After the October 1995 election, however, the incoming President will have to show interest in the reform programme and provide overall leadership it its implementation.

RECOMMENDATION 15: *Implementation of civil service reform to restructure the government and improve efficiency must be the product of political ownership and leadership at the national level.*

There is still no indication that any of the four ministries is preparing to implement the recommendations of the task force. The more likely scenario now seems to be that decisions on implementing the restructuring of the ministries will wait until after the completion of all the organisation and efficiency reviews. In our view, this would be a major mistake.

RECOMMENDATION 16: *We agree with the Secretariat's recommendation that, in normal circumstances, not later than six months after each review is completed, the accepted recommendations for strengthening and improving the efficiency of individual Ministries should be implemented. In the current context, implementation of the agreed efficiency measures should be among the top priorities of the post–election government's agenda.*

4.2 Budgetary Reform and Economic Management

The civil service reform is a medium – to long-term programme aimed at improving the overall functioning of the government. The ministries responsible for economic policy-making and the coordination and implementation of policies to improve the delivery of social service, however, require immediate strengthening. In recent months the weaknesses in revenue collection and the excessive tax exemptions have been seen as the leading problems. But the situation is actually worse than such a focus implies.

The budget process has not been taken seriously and expenditure controls remain weak, in large part because the national leadership has failed to set out clear development priorities. At the same time, all programmes are grossly underfunded. The gross under budgeting of expenditure programmes has undermined the role of the budget as the main policy instrument of the government. Mini-budgets for formalised expenditures that were not previously budgeted have become common.

Moreover, the budget is, in major respects, not transparent. For example, 'wages and salaries' in the 1994/95 budget accounted for only 16.4 and 23.2 per cent of total expenditure and recurrent expenditure respectively. Allowances which by far exceed the salaries of senior officials are budgeted under 'other goods, services and transfers', which account for 28 and 48 per cent of total expenditure respectively. As noted in Section 3 of this report, donors contribute to this lack of budget transparency when they direct funds to their own projects without integrating them into the programmes and budgets of the GoT or, in most cases, without even providing the budgetary authorities with accurate and timely information about them.

The need to meet the terms of policy conditionality – presenting a budget frame that is acceptable to the World Bank and IMF — contributes to the excessive under budgeting. The Treasury stipulates expenditure ceilings for government departments to meet the IMF/World Bank negotiated budget frame without eliminating existing expenditure programmes. The resultant lack of ownership and responsibility in the budgetary process was exemplified at the CG meeting of February 1995 when the World Bank presented estimates of the 1994/95 budget that were completely different from those presented to Parliament. The Tanzania delegation did not dispute the figures presented by the World Bank which were used to argue that the GoT did not need budgetary support because the recurrent budget was expected to record a surplus, while the budget estimate presented to Parliament recorded a deficit.

The Auditor General has routinely pointed our irregularities in government expenditures and accounting but no improvements in the budgetary process and accounting have taken place. The Treasury has lost its leadership role in controlling government expenditure. A conscious effort must therefore be undertaken to improve technical capacity in the areas of economic policy analysis, revenue forecasting and collection, budgeting, government accounting and auditing. A better working environment is also needed.

RECOMMENDATION 17: *Immediate action is required to strengthen the Ministry of Finance to enable it to prepare realistic budgets, make better projections of revenues, impose strict financial control on accounting officers, and improve accounting of government expenditure. The authority of the Treasury in budgetary matters must be respected and protected by the highest level of national political leadership.*

*The recent decision to establish an independent Revenue
Board should be used not only to create a competent revenue–
collecting institution but also, at the same time, to strengthen
the capacity for policy analysis and expenditure control in
the Treasury.*

The Planning Commission has introduced the Rolling Plan and
Forward Budget as an instrument of public investment planning.
As noted in Section 3 of this report, it has identified a 'core
investment programme' that would receive priority in the allocation
of investment resources. The exercise of reviewing and refining
the core investment programme must continue. Progress has been
made in reducing the number of investment projects from 2, 187
in 1992/93 to 1,239 in 1994/95. The number of projects is still
too large, however, and not all investment is in priority areas. Given
the high dependence on external financing, with local resources
financing less than 20 per cent of the total development budget,
cooperation with donors is essential in the development of orderly
exit mechanisms out of non-core projects. Strong leadership by
the government and transparent criteria for selecting the core public
investment programme are necessary to ensure that projects are
not classified as 'core projects' simply because external funding is
available. The impact on future recurrent budgets must also be
taken into consideration when accepting donor – funded investment
projects.

RECOMMENDATION 18: *The government needs to have a
competent aid-coordinating unit that will channel future aid
flows to priority sectors, and ensure that donor-funded
programmes and projects are fully incorporated in the
development budget and that the utilisation of donor funds
is fully accounted for.*

4.3 Social Sector Strategy

In order to design and implement a   poverty – alleviating
development programme, a strong economic management team at
the centre and in key sectoral ministries is essential. The design
and implementation of a sound social sector development strategy,
in particular, is long overdue. Both the GoT and donors are firmly
committed to the prioritisation of this sector. To maintain significant
flows of aid, the government will increasingly be required to

demonstrate that government policies and the utilisation of external resources are effective in alleviation of poverty.

The present social sector development strategy, which seems to have been mainly a product of the World Bank, working with the Planning Commission, has failed to take on board the experiences of the other donors who have been involved in the social sectors for a long time.

Sectoral ministries, in particular the Ministry of Education, have not been adequately involved in the exercise. In this connection, the Ministry of Education needs strong political and technocratic leadership, characterised by awareness of the importance of high quality basic education for all, and particularly for girls, in the promotion of a healthy and productive population. It also needs the administrative capacity to work effectively with, and coordinate policies for, local authorities and the communities that are directly managing the schools for their children. Similar strong leadership and technical capacity are also required in the Ministry of Health.

Adequate coordination in the design and implementation of social sector policies is required both within government and between government and civil society. The efforts to design a new social sector strategy are not widely known among the public, who are obviously very aware of the poor quality of health services, the falling standards of education at all levels and the lack of a dependable water supply. This reflects the fact that the strategy is a donor-driven strategy that does not have roots in Tanzanian civil society. The production of a good document with attractive graphics does not necessarily imply a policy document capable of implementation.

RECOMMENDATION 19: *In the design of social sector policy, the participation of civil society in the policy process is necessary to increase the probability of successful implementation. The social sector development strategy also requires adequate coordination between the Planning Commission, sectoral ministries, the Prime Minister's Office, and local governments and communities. It will be important to achieve early clarification of the division of responsibilities between the Ministry of Education, the Prime Minister's Office and local governments so that both central government and donor resources allocated to improve primary education* *are utilised appropriately. Local communities should be expected play a leading role in programmes to improve basic primary education and primary health care.*

It is not too late to reorient GoT planning processes in this direction.

4.4 Dealing with Corruption

Among donors and the Tanzanian public there is a widespread perception of an increase in corruption at the highest echelons of the government. Large amount of earlier balance-of-payments support provided to particular firms in the form of commodity imports and Open General License funds have not been paid for. Widespread tax exemptions that are not necessary for promoting investment continue to undermine the credibility of the GoT in the eyes of Tanzanian citizens and of donors and their taxpayers. Tanzania has traditionally attracted assistance from large numbers of donors mainly because its government and national leadership were perceived to be sincerely committed to reducing poverty. A perception that the national leadership is instead largely interested in lining its own pockets undermines the credibility of policy reforms. Both the Tanzanian public and the donors believe that the government could provide the necessary services if only it collected the taxes due. The donors are reluctant to provide balance-of-payments because they feel that it will not be used to support legitimate government activities.

RECOMMENDATION 20: Among the measures the GoT must take to restore its credibility, immediately after the election if not before, are: an increase in budget transparency; clearance of the pending issues of unpaid commodity import support and OGL cash cover; audit of the tax exemptions of the Investment Promotion Centre (IPC); reform of the Customs Department; review and amendment of the National Investment Promotion and Protection Act to separate promotion activities from regulation activities; and removal of the powers of the IPC to grant tax exemptions. In general, the design of the post-election government's policies should, wherever possible, avoid discretionary policy instruments in favour of transparent non – discretionary rules.

5. IMMEDIATE RISKS AND REQUIREMENTS

While many of the problems of aid relationships in Tanzania are common to other recipient countries, some of the features of the current Tanzanian crisis are unique to the country. In particular, the timing of the current difficulties between the Government of Tanzania and the aid donors is unfortunate. The country is in the midst of a major political transition and the first countrywide multi-party elections in its history. A newly elected government will not assume office until after the October 1995 election.

We believe, with many others, that Tanzania's long-term relations with its aid donors are at a potentially major crossroads in the year 1995. Both Tanzanians (politicians and officials) and most of the aid donors appears ready for major changes in the manner in which they interact with one another over the longer run. Realistically, however, the basic and longer-term issues in the aid relationship cannot be directly addressed until after the election. Our recommendations therefore relate primarily to the longer-term post-election prospect.

The unfortunate short-term conjuncture of the elections and the current aid crisis poses considerable immediate elements in the aid crisis as well as to the need for change on an ongoing basis and in a longer – term perspective.

As has been seen, the immediate fiscal and macroeconomic positions are quite fragile. In the budget year 1994 – 95, recurrent domestic revenue projections are below expectations and, as noted earlier, some of the expected foreign contributions have failed to materialise owing to their suspension in December 1994. At the same time, recurrent expenditures are running above the original projections. The original inflation targets for 1995 can clearly now not be met. The forthcoming parliamentary and presidential elections make an already difficult situation considerably more dangerous. The direct expenses of the election, conservatively estimated at Tsh. 20 – 25 billion, will have to appear in the 1995 – 96 recurrent budget; although there have been donor offers of support for some of them, they are bound to add to the overall budgetary pressure. In addition, election years are notorious for their expansionary effects on governmental expenditures. Political leadership in the macroeconomic realm, notably in the maintenance of budget discipline and in the control of corruption, may be weak in an environment where the President and many of those around him are required to leave office on October and key economics Ministers are engaged in electoral campaigns. Much will depend upon the credibility of the 1995 – 96 budget to be presented and approved by Parliament in June 1995, and on the capacity of the civil service to exercise the necessary controls over expenditures during the remainder of the election campaign and until the newly elected government finds its feet. It is possible to argue that these controls may be at their strongest when they are administered by the civil service, without strong political interventions; but this is by no means certain.

Should there be further loss of budgetary control in the run-up to the elections and associated increases in inflation, macroeconomic stability could quickly begin to unravel. Owners of private capital, many of whom have returned significant sums to Tanzania in recent years in response to its relative macroeconomic stabilisation, may be motivated to move their funds out again. The confidence and credibility of the entire stabilisation and reform effort, painfully built up over the course of the past nine years, could easily be lost in a burst of election-related fiscal and monetary expansion. Such a disruption of relative macroeconomic stability and loss of confidence in macroeconomic management could set the recovery effort back several years. The risks and potential costs of major macroeconomic setbacks in 1995 are too high to justify donor financial 'super-caution' at this time. The aid relationships must be improved from October 1995 onwards; but, first, it will be critical not to lose the gains already realised through previous donor-Tanzania cooperation. Donor non-project support has a particularly important role in this regard.

RECOMMENDATION 21: We urge the immediate and effective tightening of the government's fiscal controls, the presentation of a restrained and realistic government budget in June 1995, and a realistic and sympathetic response on the part of donors to the uniquely dangerous fiscal situation in the remainder of 1995. Donor financial support for election expenses and related expenditures, which has been promised, is **now a** *matter of considerable potential macroeconomic significance; it needs to be speedily provided. Resumption of the currently suspended donor non-project support of the government budget, as soon as the basic minimum requirements are met, is also a matter of great potential importance. Parliamentary approval of budget that has received the imprimatur of the IMF, and the introduction of* *an IMF shadow programme or equivalent budget control measures and commitments, should, in our view, trigger the early release of suspended balance-of-payments support and encourage the continued provision of such support for the rest of the year.*

LIST OF RECOMMENDATIONS

1. Both the Government of Tanzania and the major aid donors can and should initiate major changes in their relationships in order to restore mutual confidence and the prospect of continuing progress in Tanzania. Both should now be planning for a gradual decline in the degree of external support for Tanzania and reforms in the modes and processes through which it moves.

2. The GoT should insist on its right to prepare the first drafts of future PFPs, Letters of Intent and Letters of Development Policy, and the IFIs should honour that right. The final version of these documents must, of course, be jointly agreed and this places a requirement on government to be realistic in its approaches to these tasks.

3. The capabilities of the public administration at all levels need to be enhanced. This seems to be widely recognised and donors are anxious to help. However, here too GoT should ensure that it remains in charge and should strongly resist the imposition of technical assistance which has been common hitherto.

4. Substantial changes are needed in the operational culture of bilateral donors. Above all, they need to take far more seriously at the country level the general principles and support for local ownership espoused by policymakers in their headquarters. The gap between rhetoric and reality must be narrowed and donors must cease practices which undermine the exercise of Treasury control and other normal operations of the public administration. A greater willingness to devolve responsibilities to local offices would make it easier to harmonise donor and GoT interests.

5. (a) Taking ownership seriously entails donor willingness to withhold or delay aid until the local conditions necessary for ownership are satisfied. A culture which is willing to override ownership in order to 'do business' is inconsistent with all that has been learned about how aid can be made

more effective. A longer – term time horizon is needed than some of the donors display, for all their long past association with the country.

(b) Taking ownership seriously also entails that donors country strategies should blend both the donors' policies and those of the GoT through a process of iteration, and that consultation on these should begin at an early stage.

(c) Our recommendations on donor culture apply with particular force to the World Bank.

6. In consultation with the wider public, civil society and the donor community, the incoming GoT should urgently formulate a clear, practical, medium – to long-term development strategy for the country and be far more vigorous in seeking to impose the resulting policy and project priorities on the donors.

7. The GoT should take steps, in collaboration with donors, to achieve common arrangements for project implementation and to avoid the recent proliferation of the parallel project management systems. Increased effort should be exerted to develop Tanzanian capacity for management at all levels of programme and project implementation.

8. There is an immediate need to harmonise procedures and provide information as to appropriate donor entry points for project support in order to ensure that the coordination and policy roles of public authorities are preserved. This can be done without prejudice to the strong advantages of utilising more decentralised channels of assistance.

9. The process of arriving at the core priorities should be consultative in order to facilitate compliance at the implementation stage. In this regard it is necessary that there is harmonisation between individual donor country programmes and the agreed prioritisation. Both the Planning Commission and the Treasury should assume leading roles in ensuring this harmonisation through their annual bilateral consultations with donors.

10. To the extent that public expenditure review systems become the fulcrum of project planning and monitoring, it is imperative that the GoT should seek and obtain full information on resource commitments both from within and from outside the country. Even if the exact amounts of Direct Funds may not be available, some estimates could be provided to allow them to be taken into account in programmatic planning.

11. The central coordination role in all development endeavours ought to be that of the GoT. Two key instruments are essential in this regard: (i) a clearly articulated investment programme identifying priorities based on an overall development strategy, which is in turn converted into a Rolling Plan and Forward Budget as currently being developed; (ii) a public expenditure review system which should serve both as the basis for resource allocation and as an instrument for monitoring implementation. The implications for recurrent costs of the provisions of the investment programme must also be taken into account within such a comprehensive review system.

We cannot overemphasise the need to foster strong political commitment among the GoT and donors in adhering to the agreed prioritisation in project support, including subjecting bilateral negotiations and the drawing up of country programmes to these priorities.

12. To the extent possible, donor support should be organised sector-wide or within subsectoral project master plans developed under each ministry. In this way individual donor interventions can be harmonised along lines of common policies and strategies. Arrangements need to be in place to allow coordination across all donors involved in a specific sector. Therefore, in addition to the more general fora for exchange of information, sectoral ministries should organise specific coordinating meetings to discuss prospective programmes and review implementation, and donors should formally commit themselves to work through them.

13. Individual donor countries, through prior consultation among the relevant agencies, should combine their assistance given in the forms of new commitments and of debt relief so as to provide a basis for accurate and timely determination of financing requirements. This should also assist in determining the complete net resources envelope for budgeting purposes. First steps should be taken towards the reduction of transactions costs via the consolidation of CG and Paris Club meetings. The Tanzanian case is among the most obviously deserving of such innovation.

14. To increase the credibility of the GoT's longer-term strategies and plans, efforts will be required to stabilise government revenues and development expenditures. Donors should support such efforts, to the degree that their own rules permit,

with longer-term commitments and contingency financing arrangements to protect Tanzania programmes against unexpected adverse shocks.

15. Implementation of civil service reform to restructure the government and improve efficiency must be the product of political ownership and leadership at the national level.

16. We agree with the Secretariat's recommendation that, in normal circumstances, not later than six months after each review is completed, the accepted recommendations for strengthening and improving the efficiency of individual Ministries should be implemented. In the current context, implementation of the agreed efficiency measures should be among the top priorities of the post-election government's agenda.

17. Immediate action is required to strengthen the Ministry of Finance to enable it to prepare realistic budgets, make better projections of revenues, impose financial control on accounting officers, and improve accounting of government expenditure. The authority of the Treasury in budgetary matters must be respected and protected by the highest level of national political leadership. The recent decision to establish an independent Revenue Board should be used not only to create a competent revenue-collecting institution but also, at the same time, to strengthen the capacity for policy analysis and expenditure control in the Treasury.

18. The government needs to have a competent aid-coordinating unit that will channel future aid flows to priority sectors, and ensure that donor-funded programmes and projects are fully incorporated in the development budget and that the utilisation of donor funds is fully accounted for.

19. In the design of social sector policy, the participation of civil society in the policy process is necessary to increase the probability of successful policy implementation. The social sector development strategy also requires adequate coordination between the planning commission, sectoral ministries, the Prime Minister's Office, and local governments and communities. It will be important to achieve early clarification of the division of responsibility between the Ministry of Education, the Prime Minister's Office and local governments so that both central government and donor resources allocated to improve primarily education are utilised appropriately. Local communities should be expected to play

a leading role in programmes to improve basic primary education and primary health care.

20. Among the measures the GoT must take to restore its credibility immediately after the election if not before, are: an increase in budget transparency; clearance of the pending issues of unpaid commodity import support and OGL cash cover; audit of the tax exemptions of the Investment Promotion Centre (IPC); reform of the Customs Department; review and amendment of the National Investment Promotion and Protection Act to separate promotion activities from regulation activities; and removal of the powers of the IPC to grant tax exemptions. In general, the design of the post-election government's policies should, wherever possible, avoid discretionary policy instruments in favour of transparent non-discretionary rules.

21. We urge the immediate and effective tightening of the government's fiscal controls, the presentation of a restrained and realist government budget in June 1995, and a realistic and sympathetic response on the part of donors to the uniquely dangerous fiscal situation in the remainder of 1995. Donor financial support for election expenses and related expenditures, which has been promised, is now a matter of considerable potential macroeconomic significance; it needs to be speedily provided. Resumption of the currently suspended donor non-project support of the government budget, as soon as the basic minimum requirements are met, is also a matter of great potential importance. Parliamentary approval of a budget has received the imprimatur of the IMF, and the introduction of an IMF shadow programme or equivalent budget control measures and commitments, should, in our view, trigger the early release of suspended balance-of-payments support and encourage the continued provision of such support for the rest of the year.

Appendix

Table 1

ODA Receipts, Annual Average, 1990 – 92

	Net ODA per capita (US$ per capita)	Net ODA as % of recipient GDP
Tanzania	44	43
Sub – Sahara Africa *	44	13
Ghana	45	10
Kenya	42	12
Malawi	61	27
Uganda	39	22
Zimbabwe	50	8

* Excluding South Africa and Nigeria

Source: World Bank, African Development Indicator, 1994-95, Washington, DC

Table 2

Fiscal Performance, 1980-93 (%)

Revenue/GDP (excl. grants)	1980	1984	1985	1986	1987	1988	1989	1990	1991	1992	1993
Tanzania	17.3	15.7	15.0	13.2	13.7	13.9	17.7	18.8	19.1	21.3	20.3
Sub-Saharan Africa excl. South Africa	17.9	17.8	18.3	20.7	19.7	19.2	19.8	20.9	19.3	19.8	18.2
Ghana	6.9	8.0	11.3	13.6	14.1	13.5	13.6	11.8	13.7	11.1	16.7
Uganda	3.1	8.5	5.8	4.3	2.6	3.6	4.0	5.9	6.2	5.0	5.8
Kenya	21.9	20.2	20.0	20.3	21.0	21.1	21.8	22.4	24.7	22.3	21.8
Zimbabwe	24.1	31.6	29.2	30.2	33.0	30.8	32.4	31.0	29.3	31.3	29.3
Deficit (excl. grants)/ GDP											
Tanzania	-11.4	-7.9	-6.2	-6.9	-7.1	-8.2	-5.4	-6.1	-2.7	-2.6	
Sub-Saharan Africa excl. South Africa	-7.6	-5.5	-4.5	-5.2	-7.0	-7.7	-6.4	-6.6	-8.9	-10.3	-11.0
Ghana	-4.2	-2.1	-2.7	-0.7	-0.3	-0.7	-5.4	-5.2	-4.6	-11.2	-10.3
Uganda	-3.2	-2.4	-2.5	-2.6	-2.2	-3.6	-3.9	-5.5	-6.6	-10.6	-10.2
Kenya	-502	-5.0	-6.4	-4.6	-7.5	-5.6	-8.9	-5.7	-4.9	-4.3	-5.3
Zimbabwe	-10.9	-11.3	-9.4	-9.0	-11.8	-9.8	-9.1	-7.7	-7.5	-8.2	-6.4

Source: World Bank, African Development Indicators, 1994-95, Washington Washington, DC

Table 3

Per Capita Government Revenue (Excluding Grants), 1985-92 (US$)

	1985	1986	1987	1988	1989	1990	1991	1992	Average 1990 - 92
Ghana	40.4	59.5	53.0	50.1	49.6	49.3	62.7	48.4	53.4
Kenya	60.7	70.0	76.8	79.5	77.7	79.0	79.8	68.9	75.9
Malawi	34.9	34.8	32.0	35.8	41.7	44.0	46.6	39.5	43.3
Tanzania	48.8	29.6	21.5	20.1	21.1	19.9	24.1	22.6	22.2
Uganda	10.4	12.2	7.8	6.0	7.7	10.2	9.7	9.3	9.7
Zimbabwe	159.1	174.7	199.5	212.1	212.9	217.8	190.2	179.4	195.8

Source: Computed from data in World Bank, African Development Indicators, 1994-95, as GDP in US Dollars times government revenue as percentage of GDP, divided by population.

Chapter **2**

Development Cooperation Issues Between Tanzania and Its Aid Donors

Comments and Obsevations on the Helleiner Report

by Professor S. M. Wangwe
Executive Director
Economic and Social Research Foundation

January 1997

Comments and Observations on the Helleiner Report

Acknowledgement

These comments and observations were prepared by the Foundation under overall co-ordination of Prof. S. M. Wangwe. The Foundation appreciates the work of the two consultants: Mr. Jeremia Bulemela and Ms. Janet Mbene who worked on a substantial part of this report.

1. INTRODUCTION

The Report of the Group of Independent Advisors (The Helleiner Report) on Development Co-operation Issues between Tanzania and its aid donors was presented to government in June 1995. The government has taken the initiative to stimulate dialogue on the report among the relevant parties as one important step towards forging a new working relationship between the Government of Tanzania and the donor community and enhancing aid effectiveness.

The report has assessed and analysed the status of development co-operation between the Government of Tanzania and the official donors and has made many useful recommendations on how co-operation efforts could be made more efficient.

The purpose of this paper is to make comments and observations on the report and bring out issues we find most pertinent for improving aid relationships and enhancing aid effectiveness and efficiency of aid management.

On reading the whole report we are convinced that the report is analysing a pertinent development management problem and has put the problem in a correct perspective. The major issues of concern have been identified very ably. The report has managed to strike an admirable balance between issues on both sides (the donor side and recipient side). Reading this report in relation to recent aid evaluation reports we find that most of the findings and recommendations are consistent with the central thrust of the other evaluation reports. In particular, the report is consistent with recent aid evaluation reports on Swedish aid, Dutch aid, Danish aid and Finnish aid. The findings are generally sound and the recommendations are realistic and flow very well from the findings. This paper intends to emphasise the points we regard as most pertinent, comment on them and propose further modalities of future co-operation between Tanzania and the donors.

This paper is structured to cover issues of foreign aid relations in section 2, the question of ownership in section 3 and issues of aid co-ordination and aid effectiveness in section 4. Section 5 addresses the issue of responsibilities of the Government of Tanzania while section 6 makes general observations on the development co-operation issues.

2. FOREIGN AID RELATIONS IN TANZANIA
2.1 Crisis in Aid Relations and Subsequent Development

Background to the crisis in aid relations and its origin have been identified with failure of the government to collect counterpart funds from import support programmes, disappointing fiscal performance and intensified concern about the effectiveness of aid. This background aggravated by greater transparency and information disclosure on tax performance and tax evasion and perceptions of corruption led to strained aid relationships.

The report has correctly identified views on both sides. On the side of the donor the report indicates that donors blame Tanzania for weak performance, corruption and lack of will. On the side of Government of Tanzania the report indicates that the Government of Tanzania blames donors for making unrealistic and excessive demands on Tanzania, exerting too much influence on its development programmes and policy, not sharing information sufficiently, having no trust in Tanzania and for exerting too much senior economic managers. These observations are correct and are largely corroborated by several recent aid evaluation reports.

Indeed it is correct that aid relations have been in crisis especially at the time the report was written. Since then, however, aid relations have shown signs of improvement especially during 1996. The

50

conclusion of ESAF in November 1996 is a culmination of this trend. However, discussions of the issues raised in the Helleiner Report remain very relevant if the renewed improved relations are to be sustainable and if aid effectiveness is to be realised.

2.2 Development Co-operation Issues in Perspective

A major strength of the report is that it has provided a broad context in which development co-operation issues can be placed. In particular it has put the issue of development co-operation in at least three perspectives: that concerns about aid effectiveness are widespread; that the global trend is towards aid reduction; and how macroeconomic performance in Tanzania relates to the African countries.

2.2.1 Concerns of Aid Effectiveness Have Wider Ramifications

The report shows that the concern about aid effectiveness goes beyond Tanzania. During the late 1970s and the 1980s, aid became increasingly exposed to criticism from both the political right and the left for various and often different reasons (Riddel, 1987).[1] One response of bilateral and multilateral aid agencies was to give added emphasis to evaluation. During this period, the evaluation function became institutionalised, and most aid agencies established evaluation units within their administrative structures (Stokke, 1990). In a recent comparative study on aid effectiveness in Africa the findings from seven countries which were covered in that study indicate a great concern about aid effectiveness having fallen below expectations. As regards the perception of the effectiveness of aid a recent opinion poll in Europe revealed limited confidence in the EU's role in the allocation and management of aid (EU Newsletter November 1996). In this context about 40% of those questioned think that management of aid should he handed over to UN agencies in comparison to only 4% who favoured continued direct role of EU in the management of aid.

2.2.2 Global Foreign Aid Reduction Scenario

The report has indicated that the global trend points towards reduced aid in future. According to a recent issue of the European

---

1 Riddel, Roger, 1987, *Foreign Aid Reconsidered*, London: James Currey.

Union Newsletter (Issue 03 November 1996) Development aid is one of the 10 biggest areas of concern for European citizens. An opinion poll of some 16,346 people showed that 77.4% consider it an important element of public life. But it is also important to note that aid to poor countries in Africa, Asia and South America ranked behind concerns about unemployment, protection of the environment, fight against terrorism, guarantee of energy supplies, reducing inequality and defense of Europe's interest against the major powers. Assistance to the countries in East and Central Europe was ranked important by 73.4% of those surveyed. Considering that this is a new element in the aid equation it is quite conceivable that the lobby of this group (73.4%) could lead to reduction of aid to Africa since the absolute size of aid is not likely to increase substantially. This poll also indicated a marked fall in popular support for aid in important donor countries such as Belgium, Germany, France and United Kingdom in comparison to a similar poll conducted in 1991.

If the prospects of aid are not bright and aid reduction is a more likely scenario then it makes sense to plan development and manage the economy on the basis of the scenario of reduced aid. The report correctly observes that reduced aid need not be at the expense of Tanzania's progress provided it is planned for and managed efficiently both by donor and the Government of Tanzania.

2.2.3 Tanzania's Macroeconomic Performance in Perspective

On the basis of macro economic performance, fiscal performance and government revenues as a percentage of GDP the report concludes that Tanzania cannot be singled out as particularly lacking in revenue effort. The report correctly observes that there are considerable challenges in undertaking a transition in which economic and political liberalisations are being carried out simultaneously.

The Helleiner Report has pointed out that as reforms move beyond short-term macro economic stabilisation they become more demanding. In particular, it correctly recognises that the longer term transition from socialist to market institutions is very challenging. This observation is consistent with the experience of transition in the former socialist states in Europe.

A recent World Development Report has shown that the experience of Eastern Europe indicates that the transition from an administratively controlled economy to a market economy is more challenging than had been anticipated (World Bank, 1996). In particular, the challenges of creating appropriate institutions, new culture and attitudes and redefining an appropriate balance between state and markets have far reaching implications for transitions. The Helleiner Report correctly indicates that some of the perceived weaknesses (e.g. corruption, weak administrative capacity) are in part related to the outcomes of economic and political liberalisation.

2.3 Changing Forms of Aid: a Challenge on Evaluation of Aid Effectiveness

The changes in the forms and administration of aid constitute the most important challenge to aid evaluation in the 1990s. The changed patterns make evaluation more demanding in terms of costs and skills. One implication is a shift of level: from the project to the system, involving complex programmes, sectors, international agencies, recipient countries or sometimes even the global system.

The main challenges in the 1990s for the evaluation of development assistance, therefore, are found at two levels. First, there is a need to address the more fundamental questions related to the effectiveness and impact of aid. In order to address the increasingly pressing question of whether aid really works, within its various confines and relationships, the approaches and tools of several disciplines have to be pooled and used.

Second, to meet the managerial needs for swift and reliable information on which management decision-making in the short term can be based, improved evaluation methods adapted to the particular needs are required (Berlage and Stokke, 1992).

Project aid should continue to be phased out. Project aid has too often led to parallel administration and hence cannot easily be integrated into the national budgets. Donors should reorient their thinking in terms of budgetary support rather than project financing. Budgetary support provides a better opportunity for recipients to participate in project design and planning and gives a better guarantee that priority programmes and sectors will be identified for external assistance. However, guidelines for budgetary support, including an adequate monitoring and auditing system, have yet to be worked out. A major challenge lies in working out effective guidelines for budgetary support and putting in place accountability mechanisms that will ensure that aid and local resources are both utilised efficiently. Adequate monitoring and auditing systems will be central in restoring confidence and mutual trust between Tanzania and its official donors.

The shift in the forms of aid in favour of programme aid also implies that development assistance should focus on long-term objectives. Joint performance reviews should regularly assess the impact of the assistance in terms of the general objectives of development co-operation. In the past management of aid was paying more attention to conditions for approval of projects rather than to the requirements for successful implementation. A shift is needed therefore from an input-based to a more output- based culture in the management and implementation of development programmes.

2.4 Towards Institutional Development

The Helleiner Report correctly identifies institutional development as an area of concern for aid effectiveness. On this point the findings and recommendations of the report are consistent with other recent aid evaluation reports. We agree with all these aid evaluation reports on the emphasis they have placed on institutional development. The whole range of institutions has to be considered: public sector agencies, financial institutions, educational systems and regional and local administration. Increasing the efficiency and effectiveness of government institutions also includes attention to improvement of salaries and wages - Donor assistance to supplement salaries should be considered provided that they are clearly time-bound, that they follow explicit rules, are fully transparent, and that donor practices are harmonised. This point is elaborated in section 3.

2.5 Aid and Self Reliance

An important issue that deserves further emphasis when analysing Tanzania's foreign aid relations relates to the fact that Tanzania does not have an explicit aid policy and strategy for guiding the mobilisation and administration of external resources. It is worth noting in this connection that the Arusha Declaration had implicitly put forward the following three - fold criteria on seeking and accepting aid:
- Foreign aid should not endanger the country's independence and freedom to make key policy decisions regarding the economy and the future of its society.
- Aid was to be consistent with the policy of socialism and self-reliance i.e. complementing rather than substituting for local efforts and initiatives towards the declared policy objectives.
- The country's ability to repay was to be considered seriously.

These criteria are valid under the current circumstances. The problem is that these criteria do not seem to have been observed in practice. Towards the end of the 1970s and thereafter it became clear that Tanzania did not observe the criteria it had set for itself. This violation or non-observance of the set criteria has contributed considerably to the outcome, in terms of aid-relations and less than satisfactory effectiveness of aid. There is thus urgent need for reviewing this matter and taking a position considering the current donor aid fatigue.

3. THE QUESTION OF OWNERSHIP
3.1 Importance of Local Ownership
The importance of national 'ownership' of development projects and programmes, however great their external inputs, derives from its inherent appropriateness and efficacy. This fact is emphasised in the Helleiner Report as well as the various donor agency reports. According to these findings, projects and programmes that are locally owned by those who implement them have proved more likely to work and to be sustained. These observations are very valid and warrant high priority to be accorded to issues of enhancing local ownership of development policy and programmes.

3.2 Dimensions of "Ownership"
The report has correctly observed that the word "ownership" is used loosely. The report then proceeds to make an important contribution in pointing to several dimensions of "ownership".

According to the Helleiner Report, there are various indicators of ownership of development projects and programmes. They include factors such as:
- Whose objectives does it reflect- the recipient government's or the donor's?
- Who initiated, designed and evaluated it?
- To what extent do leading members of the government support controversial policies in public speeches?
- How vigorous is the government in 'selling' them to the wider public?
- To what extent has the public been consulted in the preparatory stages of project/programme in order to reach agreement?
- To what extent has the responsibility for the project been vested upon those it most affects?

The report has rightly suggested that ownership must mean that the final decisions rest with the recipient government.

3.3 Low Level of Ownership

According to the Helleiner Report with the exception of a few examples (e.g. the Integrated Roads Programme), the ownership of aid development programmes and projects situation in Tanzania is at present unsatisfactory. The findings of several other aid evaluation reports are consistent with the observation that both donors and Government of Tanzania have contributed to the problem of limited local ownership of development projects/programmes.

Various recent evaluation reports have also expressed concern on this issue (e.g. Swedish, Finnish and Danish). Although Swedish aid policy in recent years is reported to be aimed at increasing the role of the recipient country, according to aid evaluation report, (SASDA Report) this has been difficult to achieve due to the weak capacity of Tanzania both economically and institutionally. As a result many of the projects/programmes funded by Sweden have been donor-driven particularly with regard to financing and personnel. Consequently, responsibility for implementation has increasingly been taken away from the Government of Tanzania. FINNIDA Aid Evaluation Report also admits to a low local ownership of its aid assistance to Tanzania in the past. The Report states "In principle, Tanzania is involved in all phases of project cycle. All the requests come from Tanzanian side etc. All the missions are carried out by joint teams as well as the selection of implementing agencies of projects". The report on Finnish aid however proceeds to observe that the practice is different. Many difficulties arise at the implementation phase. The report concludes that the fact that implementation takes place within the local structures does not necessarily mean that implementation is not 'donor-driven'. The report observes that there are reported cases where intrusive donor conditionalities were imposed even at the level of implementation (FINNIDA, 1994). The findings of these aid evaluation reports are applicable to most donor - Tanzania relations.

3.3.1 Ownership of the Policy Agenda

The report has pointed out that many initiatives originate with donors, with only limited policy guidance from the Government of Tanzania. An example is given of a key policy document, the Policy Framework Paper (PFP) of 1994, which the report says appears to be a collaborative effort but ownership was dampened by two factors. First, the original draft was prepared in Washington.

Second, after it was agreed the World Bank introduced new conditionalities during the negotiation of a new structural credit. We concur with the recommendation of the report that the Government of Tanzania should insist on preparing first drafts of PFPs and related policy statements and that final versions should be jointly agreed.

The implication of this recommendation is that the Government of Tanzania will need to mobilise its capacities in the central and sectoral ministries and key policy institutions such as the Bank of Tanzania and other capacities outside government to make inputs to the PFP and other policy documents. The capacities for policy analysis and economic management may be limited but the limited existing capacities need to be mobilised and utilised more fully. Effectiveness of local capacities would be enhanced further if reparations were to be made in good time so that preparation of important policy documents is not done in a rush to meet very short deadlines.

This task should be regarded as a normal and regular process in the Government economic management system and not as an emergency. This implies that institutional machinery for this process will need to be put in place. Inter-ministerial Team of experts should be setup for this task. This team would have the mandate to mobilise technical support from elsewhere within or outside the government.

3.3.2 Absorptive Capacity

The implementation of a number of aid projects/programmes demonstrates the failure to realise counterpart funding and local personnel from the GoT as earlier anticipated. In other words, the Government of Tanzania often failed to honor its commitments. This situation could be explained by at least two factors. First, aid projects and commitments have tended not to be programmed with the full consideration of the government's absorptive capacity and its ability to mobilise local resources to match the aid resources. Secondly, there has been lack of a political constituency demanding the accountability of aid administrators and authorities in the failures. In effect, Tanzanian authorities are not pressurised by the local political constituency or by donors into being more realistic about their ability to mobilise and commit domestic resources. Consequently, there is a tendency of over-commitment on the part of the Government of Tanzania, which leads to unsustainability of aid projects and programmes. In the final respect, the local ownership of aid efforts is undermined.

If the absorptive capacity is so limited, the question which arises whether there has been too much aid or not. It appears that this limitation of aid-absorptive capacity has a bearing on two factors, namely, the type of aid and its administration. Aid has been coming in terms of projects or programmes for which parallel administrative machineries have been established. Such parallel machineries have formed island projects with their own administrative systems. These machineries have exerted pressure on the existing government administrative machinery in at least two ways: by employing a number of public servants in these projects; and/or by demanding too much time and energy from officials in the respective ministries. This fact has tended to erode rather than build the Government's limited capacity. As such, aid administration on the part of Government of Tanzania has taken on a form more consistent with capacity using or depleting rather than capacity building. In a situation of low government capacity for economic management, it seems logical to allocate more aid towards building that capacity. The challenge is how the aid projects can be administered in future to make less intensive use of the limited capacity of the government's administrative machinery and whether the allocation of aid can be shifted in favour of capacity building in areas where it is limited (e.g. in economic management).

3.3.3 Capacity Building

Some aid programmes are operated with little consultation, co-ordination and collaboration with the related activities within government and sometimes within the same ministry or even department. In view of this situation it is suggested that to the extent possible, donor-supported projects should be located within the respective ministerial departments or in other relevant national institutions. If these institutions are deemed weak, then a case for enhancing their capacities could be made instead of operating projects in parallel structures. It has been observed that the Management Information Systems (MIS) within the government machinery are weak; a problem which is itself characteristic of a low capacity for economic management. Capacity building needs should therefore be understood as a process rather than as an event or an isolated activity in a project. Capacity building in one project is often influenced by activities outside the project. This suggests that coordination with relevant activities should be given greater attention. This would require the development of a national framework to guide the capacity building process.

Capacity building programmes should continue to be directed towards the government's leadership role in economic management of various sectors in terms of improving policy formulation, monitoring and evaluation. Besides, planning, budgeting and accountancy management should be strengthened as a prerequisite for greater accountability and local ownership of aid efforts. However, when introducing new procedures, adequate transition periods should be allowed for, during which targeted training for the relevant Government departments and the field office should be undertaken. The activities, which should be undertaken during this transition, should be planned jointly by the donors and government. It is imperative to recognise that capacity requirements are dynamic, changing with challenges of economic management. As such the government should develop a framework for reviewing its capacity to manage the economy in a continuous manner in a changing environment.

Furthermore, capacity building should also include the strengthening of the local government, the regional and district administrations, community-based organisations and NGOs for the purpose of promoting the society's actual involvement and participation in development at all levels. Greater efforts should be made towards extending capacity building initiatives to these levels. This could be done by preparing a separate programme for capacity building at local levels and non-government development agencies distinct from capacity projects in the ministries.

3.3.4 Conducive Working Conditions

One major factor that reduces the effectiveness of capacity building projects in economic management is the unconducive working conditions especially the unrealistically low levels of wages and salaries. This point has been recognised in the Helleiner report consistent with findings in other recent aid evaluation reports. The perception of this threat and unfavourable working conditions continue to strangle civil service reform efforts and make it difficult for both the staff and institutions to give adequate attention to the longer-term demands of economic management. The existing capacities cannot be fully utilised under these conditions. It will be necessary to pay special attention to the civil service reform components that deal with the working conditions of civil servants (including their remunerations) and integrate the civil service into the whole programme of capacity building in economic management.

3.3.5 Building the Capacity of Local Firms

In order to build the competitiveness of local firms in the production of goods and services, donor-recipient inter-firm cooperation arrangements (with technologically more advanced firms in donor countries), should be encouraged. Although this issue is not raised in the Helleiner Report we believe it is consistent with the spirit of that report. The nature of inter-firm cooperative arrangements should reflect the relative capabilities of the partnering firms. These arrangements should be designed along the lines of sound commercial principles, technological capability and competitiveness on the side of the partners. Under these arrangements, business negotiations would determine the extent to which the interests of the partnering parties are met. In such cases, certain conditionalities relating to procurement from donor countries can play a positive role in sustaining the business partnerships. For instance, if such tied procurement enhances resource mobilisation and necessary infrastructure support from the donor country and Tanzania in the interest of both partner firms or enhances technological capability of the weaker partner it may well be in the business interest of both firms to co-operate.

3.3.6 Technical Assistance

The Helleiner Report has observed that the experience of technical co-operation in Tanzania is consistent with wider findings on technical co-operation in Africa as revealed in a recent UNDP report (1993) on this subject. We concur with this observation. It may also be added that the observations made in the report are consistent with the findings of recent aid evaluation reports in Tanzania. These reports have noted that while the operational component of technical assistance has been relatively successful the training component has performed poorly, a factor that has undermined ownership and sustainability.

Technical assistance (TA) is often allocated to fill the current operating positions. For this backstopping function, they have generally been effective. These short-term pressures to get the work done, however, have tended to divert attention from the longer-term objectives of capacity building (of individuals and institutions). There is need both for the operational functions of TA and the requirements for local capacity building. The terms of references in respect of which task the TA is being engaged to perform should be clearly stipulated. Such terms of references should be agreed upon between the donor and the recipient institutions with greater weight being placed on the latter. It should also be clear that the evaluation of performance would reflect the content of such terms of reference.

The question of on-the-job training should be approached in a broader and more comprehensive manner. The lack of on the-job training in the civil service is not only found where foreign staffs are engaged but it is also prevalent among the national staff. High level civil servants hardly have time, because of pressure from operational demands, to train junior staff on-the-job. For some projects, it is felt that too much emphasis is put on formal training as a means to achieve capacity building (e.g. through scholarships). Relatively less attention is given to on-the-job training. The civil service reform therefore should address this problem in a more comprehensive manner.

Another option in respect of enhancing the effectiveness of technical assistance in capacity building and policy reforms is to address the issue of technical assistance by introducing prices in that market and untying TA from other aid items. TA has been regarded as "free" and this has sometimes been engaged to replace local human resources rather than complement them. The new pricing system should be introduced in such a way that the TA is paid out of the budget of the user. At macro-level, the TA should be allowed to compete for available foreign aid and domestic resources along with other forms of aid and other claimants of domestic resources. The TA bundle should be unpackaged and such unpackaging of TA should start by clearly making a provision for local institutions to request for the various TA components separately (e.g. personnel, equipment, training) without any prejudice. In effect TA should be completely untied. Various aid evaluation reports have revealed that in practice most donors find it difficult to accept the untying of TA to other aid packages. But we are of the opinion that this should be an area of serious negotiations between Tanzania and donors to ensure complementarity between TA and local technical capabilities.

In order to enhance the personnel-related effectiveness in technical cooperation, it is recommended that the practice of having experts and project staff outside the regular established posts should be reviewed critically or rather abolished. The vacant posts should instead be filled by recruiting operating staff to fill the line posts. This suggestion requires that experts be integrated into the national administration. The fact that the post is established in this way will not only make the determination of TA personnel needs easier but will also make sustainability more likely. The salary and benefit requirements which go with the post would be met from the national budget while topping-up could be negotiated separately under some technical assistance arrangements. Salaries of these experts could be supplemented with transparency. This way they would work with nationals as peers; be subordinate to some co- workers and at the same time be the supervisors of others. Alternatively, TAP and workers of aid agencies could take positions in line ministries rather than being under parallel administrative systems. This arrangement could make experts feel more accountable to the government rather than the donor and would make the government pay greater attention to the real needs of the experts as their presence will have budgetary implications under the new arrangements.

The threshold is that technical assistance should play the role of a temporary gap filler or training for purposes of capacity building. In other words, technical assistance should complement rather than replace local capabilities. It is through this way that, capacity building in local institutions could be enhanced.

3.3.7 Collaboration in Preparing Country Programmes

The process of preparing aid policies and strategies and country programmes by donors should be done in collaboration with the recipient countries. The Helleiner Report continues to suggest that this process should be improved in terms of taking into account the goals and priorities of the recipient and the donor. This observation is consistent with concerns raised in recent aid evaluation reports (e.g. Dutch, Danish, Swedish). The developments in this direction show some positive signs. For instance, the new Danish Aid Strategy (1994) has recognised the need for participation by partners in recipient country administrations and civil society in the design and implementation of the country programmes. The participatory process starts with inviting local experts to prepare analytical papers on the country's situation and needs. This is followed by consultations with other local partners and the Danish "resource base". In the case of formulating the Tanzania country aid strategy the process started with the invitation of a group of Tanzanian experts in 1994 to draft discussion papers on sectors and crosscutting issues which were deemed relevant for Danish assistance. The drafts were discussed in a seminar on 10 April 1995 in which broad participation was drawn from diverse sectors in society. The seminar made proposals on sectors to be retained in the country strategy. This type of seminar had not been organised before by DANIDA or any other donor. It marks commendable progress in the process of consultations in the formulation of the strategy for co-operation. The seminar resolved that the following steps would need to be taken: -

(i)   Clarification of the extent to which individual sectors have the potential for achieving overall development objectives;

(ii) The sector's capacity for absorption of resources in the form of programme assistance;

(iii) Post-Danish aid experience in the sector;

(iv) An assessment of the comparative advantage of Danish resource base; and

(v)   An assessment of Tanzania's priorities in relation to the future Danish aid to Tanzania.

The outcome of this seminar was discussed in another seminar in Denmark in which the Danish resource base participated. On the basis of all these inputs the Danish side launched discussions with the Tanzanian authorities on the selection of sectors and forms of Danish aid. This formed the basis for the draft country strategy, which was discussed at the annual aid consultations.

The process of planning and programming of the development projects and programmes is riddled with uncertainties of resource commitments (especially from donors). Donors could facilitate this process by providing full information on resource commitments, say over a 3-5 year period, including making estimates of direct funds that would allow a higher degree of confidence in the planning and programming of these projects.

3.3.8 Towards Policy Direction

The report observes that the passivity of the Government of Tanzania and the aid dependence syndrome have created an environment which permits most initiatives to originate from the donors. We agree with the report on this point and that the government should and can impose much more authority on the donors than it does at present. The report proceeds to observe that such action would require strong political leadership and a clear consensus on the desirable direction of development of Tanzania and its priorities.

Since the Helleiner Report came out in June 1995 developments in this direction have been encouraging. First, the political leadership of the Third Phase Government has shown concern about improving aid relationships between Tanzania and its donors.

The will to improve aid effectiveness and to formulate domestic policies has shown positive developments. Recent initiatives to prepare various sectoral policies (e.g. agricultural policy, industrial policy, mining policy, education and training policy) are steps in the right direction. Development in crafting a long term development vision for Tanzania which is currently in progress under the overall co-ordination of the Planning Commission are promising and should form the basis for preparing medium term and long term development strategies.

4. DONOR CO-ORDINATION AND AID EFFECTIVENESS

The report has expressed concern about aid co-ordination, current arrangements and further dimensions of aid co-ordination and effectiveness.

The report makes valid observations on donor co-ordination and aid effectiveness as follows:

- Failure to match various interests with agreed and co-ordinated priorities;
- Proliferation of projects and parallel project management system
- Limited government capacity;
- Harmonisation of procedures and information;
- Lack of co-ordination among government agencies;
- Need to develop a vision;
- Harmonisation between donor country programmes and agreed prioritisation;
- Information on resource commitments both within and outside;
- Need to organise sector-wide project master plans and make arrangements to allow co-ordination across all donors involved in a specific sector;
- Combining aid commitments with debt relief to determine financing requirements;
- Stability of the joint development effort and enhancing credibility of government policies and programmes;

We are in agreement with the above observations made in the

report. Four points are selected for further comments and observations.

4.1 Sector-wide Co-ordination

The Helleiner Report has rightly proposed that to the extent possible, donor support should be organised sector wide or within subsectoral project master plans developed under each ministry. In this way individual donor interventions can be harmonised along the lines of common policies and strategies. Arrangements need to be in place to allow co-ordination across all donors involved in a specific sector. Therefore, in addition to the more general fora for exchange of information, sectoral ministries should organise specific co-ordination meetings to discuss prospective programmes and review implementation, and donors should formally commit themselves to work through them.

While overall aid co-ordination is expected to be spearheaded by the central ministries (Finance and Planning Commission) sectoral ministries will need to take the lead in co-coordinating their specific sectors. The recent initiative that the Ministry of Education and Culture has taken to form an Education Sector Co-ordination Committee is a step in the right direction.

Recognising that the concerns of education go beyond the preview of the Ministry of Education and Culture the Sector Co-ordinating Committee was constituted to include members from related ministries (e.g. Finance, Prime Minister's Office, Science and Technology and Higher Education, Civil Service Department, Labour and Youth Development). The composition of the Committee is a good example of how local capacities from more than one Ministry can be used to enhance sectoral analysis and policy analysis. The Committee discusses all matters relating to education sector policies and development programmes. Various donor initiatives, studies and proposals are studied by the Committee and decided upon in the light of the sectoral policies and programmes. Initiatives for education related policy studies and research are guided by this Committee. The Committee is serviced by a small secretariat, which draws technical support from local capacities in existing local institutions (e.g. universities, other institutions of higher learning, consulting firms, research institutes). This initiative is an important step towards effective sector-wide co-ordination.

The following issues should be considered, as they will contribute greatly to improving the current arrangements for aid co-ordination: -

- Strengthening of the prioritisation process based on consensus through the empowerment of the grass root institutions to enable them plan and implement their own development agenda.
- Changing the perception of aid accountability and transparency. Currently donors perceive accountability and transparency as issues binding only the recipient. They too should feel and be held accountable to the recipient on the basis of negotiated and agreed criteria.

4.2 Linking New Aid Commitments to Debt Relief

One important area that the Helleiner Report addresses relates to the need for individual donor countries to co-ordinate their assistance, which they provide in the form of new aid flows with what they offer in the form of debt relief. The report notes that currently there are two distinct fora (Consultative Groups and Round Tables, and Paris Club) involved and disjunction in information may occur under such an arrangement due to the difference in the timing of the two meetings.

On the basis of this finding the report recommends that individual donor countries, through prior consultation among the relevant agencies, should combine their assistance given in the forms of new commitments and of debt relief so as to provide a basis for accurate and timely determination of financing requirements. This should also assist in determining the complete net resource envelope for budgeting purposes. First steps should be taken towards the reduction of transaction costs via the consolidation of Consultative Groups and Paris Club meetings. The Tanzania case is among the most obviously deserving of such innovation.

Considering the extent to which debt servicing has become a burden in the implementation of development programmes any debt relief is likely to be a most direct way of releasing domestic resources for financing of development programmes in ways, which are not accompanied by all the problems of project implementation, which the report has identified. That kind of aid (debt relief) would be equivalent to the more flexible forms of aid such as budgetary support or balance of payments support.

4.3 Demand for Co-ordination

The Helleiner Report has correctly pointed out that there is a mismatch between interest of individual donor and government agencies on the one hand and agreed and co-ordinated priorities on the other.

A major constraint to the achievement of aid coordination is the lack of demand for it. A local constituency demanding an improved aid co-ordination is only beginning to emerge. Also interest in the possibility of playing one donor against another and getting access to donor funds have delayed the move towards aid coordination. For instance, some recipients may know very well that aid coordination would demand a greater justification of their aid requests. Besides, on the side of the donors, there are indications that some donors are not keen to be co-ordinated, as co-ordination is perceived to be constraining to freedom of action on their part.

4.4 Towards a National Aid Strategy

The findings and recommendations made by the report on aid coordination are pertinent and realistic. It should be emphasised further that aid coordination, however, remains a primary responsibility of the recipient. Effective aid coordination can be achieved by formulating a clear national aid strategy. Some of the key elements of a national aid strategy would include: the national objectives, strategies and priorities; an articulation of roles of the recipient, donors and implementing agencies; a stipulation of modes of disbursement and accountability; and areas of focus and concentration.

5. RESPONSIBILITIES OF THE GOVERNMENT OF TANZANIA

5.1 Need to Articulate a National Vision

The Helleiner Report has emphasised that Tanzania's national leadership needs to articulate a development vision. The emphasis is well deserving. This vision is important both to improve effective utilisation of foreign aid and to mobilise and utilise domestic resources efficiently to promote poverty-alleviating growth. The objective of the broad-based development vision will aim at commitment to all basic tenets of our development, such as universal and relevant primary education, access to basic primary health care and clean water for all, local community participation, and broad-based agricultural and rural development. A clear commitment in deeds to a regulatory framework which is supportive to the private sector in general and rural households in particular is also necessary.

Articulation of a development vision should be accompanied by adequate design of sound policies and the building of an effective administrative and institutional machinery capable of implementing and reviewing development policies and communicating with and learning from those affected by these policies. Vision also requires a recognition of the resource constraints facing the government, and the mobilisation and allocation of financial resources in the priority sectors. To donors that are interested in supporting poverty-alleviation and broad-based development, government effort in revenue collection and expenditure allocations to sectors that increase the capacity of the poor are the greatest measure of a government commitment to the promotion of development.

5.2 Strengthening Government Machinery

There is a general consensus that the government machinery is at present very weak. The formulation and implementation of government economic policy and overall economic management are undoubtedly in disarray.

The current weakness of the public administration has been caused by measures taken in the late 1960s and 1970s to promote rapid socialist development. These measures including extensive nationalisation of commercial enterprises, decentralisation of central government, the removal of local government, villagisation, abolition of cooperatives and the introduction of multi-purpose crop authorities, expansion of the party bureaucracy, intensive politicisation of the civil service etc. overextended the role of government beyond its administrative capacity and resource availability, while at the same time undermining discipline, work ethics and the link between responsibility and accountability. (With) The fall in the purchasing power of wages and salaries and the development of parallel markets eroded the morale and morality of the civil service contributing further to the inefficiency of the government in the delivery of public service.

To improve government performance is a matter of utmost priority at the moment. This can be achieved through:

5.2.1 Civil Service Reform

The improvement of government performance is to be pursued by implementing a civil service reform because the civil service lies at the centre of all government operations and efficiency or lack of it influences how the whole government machinery performs. The civil service reform envisaged is one that has a smaller, affordable, well paid, efficient and effectively performing civil service working to implement redefined policies and strategies for national economic development and delivery of public services.

It is noted in the report that, the main problem facing the civil service reform and one which is likely to undermine its implementation, is the fact that it appears to lack 'political ownership' at the national level. The whole exercise is seen as one of retrenchments with the possible accompanying 'golden hand shake' rather than as a programme of increased efficiency to deliver better public services.

Another problem associated with the civil service reform and its focus on retrenchments and compensation of retrenchees is that, the government has not saved nor laid the foundation for improving the efficiency of the civil service. To ensure that the civil service reform achieves its objectives, the Secretariat of the Civil Service Reform Commission has been conducting organisation and efficiency reviews, which streamline the government structure. However, there is still no clear system for ensuring response or implementation of the recommendations. For example, by mid-April 1995, the Secretariat had not received the response from PMOs office and the Planning Commission to recommendations sent to them in December 1994. The Report noted with surprise the absence of a quick response, given that the Secretariat is composed of Principal Secretaries (among others) of some of the ministries reviewed and as such it should be easy for them to respond to issues that are already familiar to them.

Without the national leadership providing the general guidelines and taking the political responsibility for the difficult decisions required, the civil service reform may end up being an exercise in futility. The report has proposed that it would be imperative for the new President to show interest in the reform programme at hand to provide overall leadership in its implementation.

Implementation of the civil service reform to restructure the government and improve efficiency must be a result of political ownership and leadership at the national level. It has been proposed that in normal circumstances, not later than six months after each review is completed, the accepted recommendations for strengthening and improving the efficiency of individual Ministries should be implemented. Implementation of the agreed measures should be among the top priorities of the government. We are in agreement with the findings and recommendations made regarding the civil service reform.

5.2.2 Budgetary Reforms and Economic Management

The Helleiner Report has observed that the budget has not been taken seriously and expenditure controls remain weak. At the same time, all programmes are grossly underfunded. The gross over budgeting of programmes has undermined the role of the budget as the main policy instrument of the government. The frequency of mini- budgets to formalise expenditures not previously budgeted is common. All these point to the failure of the national leadership to set out clear development priorities.

In major respects the budget is not transparent. This is noted as one of the contributing factors to the practice of some donors directing funds to their own projects without integrating them into the programmes and budgets of the Government of Tanzania or, in most cases, even failing to provide the budgetary authorities with accurate and timely information about them. It is noted that the need to meet terms of policy conditionality in a budget frame acceptable to the World Bank/IMF contributes to the excessive under budgeting. The demands to abide within the budget ceilings override reason in realistic budgeting.

The report has consequently recommended that immediate action is required to strengthen the Ministry of Finance to enable it to prepare realistic budgets, make better projections of revenues, impose strict financial control on accounting officers, and improve accounting of government expenditure. The authority of the Treasury in budgetary matters must be respected and protected by the highest level of national political leadership. The recent decision to establish an independent Revenue Board should be used not only to create a competent revenue -collecting institution but also, at the same time, to strengthen the capacity for policy analysis and expenditure control in the Treasury. We agree to these findings and recommendations. In fact, since then the Tanzania Revenue Authority has been formed and started its operations officially in July 1996. The other aspects of strengthening capacity for policy analysis and expenditure control in the Treasury are still challenges to be faced urgently.

Adequate co-ordination is needed in design and implementation of social sector policies both within government and between government and civil society. The society most affected by the poor social services is not aware of efforts to design a new social sector strategy. This reflects the fact that the strategy is donor-driven. This may have implications for its implementation. However, it is not too late to reorient Government of Tanzania planning processes in this direction.

5.2.3 Dealing with Corruption

Among donors and the Tanzanian public the report points out, there is a widespread perception of an increase in corruption at the highest echelons of the government. The issue of large amounts of earlier balance of payments support provided to particular firms in the form of commodity imports and Open general License funds have not been paid yet. Widespread tax evasions that are still existing etc have undermined the credibility of the Government of Tanzania in the eyes of Tanzanian citizens, donors and their taxpayers, the report observed.

Among the measures the Government of Tanzania must take to restore its credibility immediately are: an increase in budget transparency; clearance of the pending issues of unpaid commodity import support and OGL cash cover; audit of the tax exemptions of the Investment Promotion Centre (IPC); reform of the Customs Department; review and amendment of the National Investment Promotion and Protection Act to separate promotion activities from regulation activities; and removal of the powers of the IPC to grant tax exemptions. In general, the design of the post- election government's policies should, wherever possible, avoid discretionary policy instruments in favour of transparent non-discretionary rules.

The biggest challenge facing the government at the moment is that of salvaging its credibility in view of the gross mismanagement in its administration. The issue of corruption is a thorn in the people's flesh and has become very irksome to the external donor community. The recent move by the President to set up a special task force to look into incidence of corruption and identify major areas reeking with the evil as well as coming up with recommendations on how best to curb corruption is a positive step in the right direction. The report (the Warioba Report) is out and has been made public. What is awaited is the implementation of the recommendations of the task force.

In view of the tax collections and exemptions, this problem has been taken care of with the installation of the Tanzania Revenue Authority. Tax exemption will not be considered unless it is scrutinised and recommended by the Revenue Authority, which is an autonomous body for implementation and overseeing revenue collection in the country.

The structure and functions of IPC have been studied and the proposals to effect changes towards making it more autonomous and making its role more facilitating and promotional (have been made).

6. GENERAL OBSERVATIONS OF THE DEVELOPMENT CO-OPERATION ISSUES
6.1 Aid Dependence
The degree of Tanzania's dependence on aid has increased over time in spite of the declared objective of the Arusha Declaration on the realisation of self-reliance. This fact raises concern and underscores the need for an aid strategy focusing on the gradual and smooth reduction of aid as a vital resource in the development agenda. In this point we are in full agreement with the report that the most realistic policy option would be to plan for better utilisation of aid resources and the ultimate phasing out of aid dependence over time. This strategy should be a top priority primarily for Tanzania with support from her partners in development. There are at least three policy implications: more emphasis needs to be placed on domestic resource mobilisation; paying greater attention to more efficient utilisation of the local natural and human resources; and giving priorities to national capacity building especially in the management of the economy. In particular, domestic resource mobilisation should place emphasis on three fronts: budget revenue collection efforts and budget management more generally; savings mobilisation; and export development and promotion.

6.2 Aid Conditionality
6.2.1 Conditionalities in Terms of Procurement
Conditionalities in terms of procurement policy or politics are often donor-driven and are characterised by much asymmetry since such conditionalities seem not to be negotiated by both parties on an equal footing. Aid conditionalities of whatever form should be geared towards improving the effectiveness of aid programmes; including the attainment of sustainability. It is in this context that aid conditionalities should be discussed and agreed upon by both partners in development (the recipients and donors) and should be implemented based on the need to enhance the effectiveness of aid while satisfying the interests of both partners.

6.2.2 Distortion of Aid Tying

Distortion of aid tying is well known (e.g. high price products, inappropriate technology and problem of proliferation). However, there could be a positive side to it if it is designed to create and enhance sustainable business relations between business communities in the donor and recipient countries. Relative benefits should be determined within the framework of normal business negotiations typical of any business practice. The mutuality of interests between the business partners could enhance the mobilisation of resources through the lobbying for supportive resources and infrastructures from the political systems of donors and recipients alike. In this context, bidding procedures which favour the continuation of healthy business relationships deserve encouragement. The guiding principle here is: whose interests are at stake when procurement conditionalities are put in place. Could such conditionalities be designed in a way, which promotes the appearance of other indicators of success?

6.3 Accountability and Transparency

6.3.1 In view of the above observations, there is a need to broaden the narrow definition of aid accountability and transparency to also include the donor, accountability and transparency in the management and control of aid should be a two-way process. In other words, the aid recipient should be accountable to the donor; at the same time the donor should also be accountable to the recipient (if greater effectiveness of aid has to be achieved). The two parties should agree on goals and targets and on the conditions for achieving them. These conditions should form the basis of conditionality and accountability.

6.3.2 The capacities to plan and manage development have been eroded during the structural adjustment period as a result of deteriorating working conditions in the recipient countries (while the donors' development agenda has expanded ahead of the capacity of some donor agencies). Developing the conditions and capacities of recipient institutions in the public and private sectors deserves greater attention in future. This also entails strengthening the Government of Tanzania's management information system (MIS) as well as accounting and resources management systems.

6.3.3 Donors could do more to address the issue of accountability and transparency especially in terms of capacity building. Technical assistance provided has mainly been part of specific projects or programme financed without specifically being aimed at redressing the institutional capacity weaknesses. In order to speed up implementation, donors are tempted to perform some of the functions of the recipient countries (Bossyut and Laporte, 1994). This tends to threaten progress towards local capacity building and the local ownership of the development programmes.

6.4 Capacity for Economic Management

Tanzania has often had difficulties in meeting its commitments in donor funded programmes. The failure to honour commitments has contributed considerably to eroding the confidence and trust the donors can place on Tanzania. In order to resume aid relations in which there is mutual trust and confidence this situation needs to be rectified. Failure to meet commitments can be traced to the weaknesses in budget management, absence of clear prioritisation of commitments, limitations in the capacity to design realistic programmes or weaknesses in the monitoring and accountability mechanisms.

The Helleiner Report and all other recent aid evaluation reports are in agreement that utilisation of aid could have been more effective. Could it be that aid effectiveness is low while the utilisation of domestic resources is effective? Or are both aid and domestic resources subjected to inadequate levels of effectiveness?

It is sometimes argued that aid is perceived to be a free or less costly resource than domestic resources, suggesting that foreign aid resources are utilised less efficiently and the design of aid projects is therefore done with less care. To the extent this perception is tenable then the shift away from project aid to programme aid, sectoral aid, budgetary support or balance of payments support is a logical solution to this problem.

The shift to sectoral aid or budgetary support is supported by recent experiences with project aid and the problems associated with it.

In particular, there are problems of proliferation of projects, proliferation of different donor procedures, great demands on administrative capacity and time and energy of economic management and other problems associated with parallel co-financing.

The shift towards sectoral aid or budget support is more

consistent with co-financing arrangements whereby several donor resources and domestic resources would be allocated jointly to priority sectoral activities or activities approved in a well-managed budget. This arrangement would reduce administrative demands by limiting the number of separate aid relationships Tanzania has to manage and would facilitate harmonisation and standardisation of aid procedures.

Management of sectoral aid and budgetary support, however, demands a greater capacity for sectoral planning and management and budget management. This is an area which calls for immediate action to put in place mechanisms for co-ordination of sectoral plans and activities and mechanisms for effective budget management. Enhancing the capacity for budget management and sectoral co-ordination can be effected in the short term through mobilisation and effective utilisation of domestic capabilities within any one Ministry (or government department), across related Ministries (inter-ministerial teams of experts) and outside the government system. In particular, more effective utilisation of capacities in universities and research institutes, other institutions of higher learning, NGOs, private sector and consulting firms can augment the limited capacity of the government machinery in budget management and sector-wise economic management. Technical assistance from outside the country would be selectively invited to fill gaps in local capacities, i.e. complement local technical capabilities.

Mobilisation and effective utilisation of economic managers and supportive experts is a major challenge in civil service reform. In particular, the components relating to pay reform, personnel management, organisation and efficiency reviews and capacity building and training deserve highest priority.

To the extent that foreign aid resources are interlinked with domestic resources in intricate ways, much of what the Helleiner Report has found and recommended in respect of the effectiveness of aid is relevant to the question of effective utilisation of domestic resources too. In our opinion, the analyses of aid relationships provide very useful insights on the broader problem of budget management, sectoral co-ordination, and the overall issue of enhancing the capacity for policy analysis and economic management. The challenge now is at the level of implementation of the recommendations for the report.

REFERENCES

Bagachwa, M.S.D., G. Mjema, I. Shitundu and S.M. Wangwe. *A study on Aid Effectiveness: the case of Danish Aid.* ERB/ESRF/CDR. January 1997.

Bossuyt, J. and G. Laporte. 'Policy Management Brief'. *European Centre for Development Policy,* No. 3. (December 1994).

Bol, D. "The Effectiveness of Aid Intentions". Paper presented at Conference on Aid Effectiveness in Tanzania, Dar es Salaam, Tanzania.(January 1995).

Doriye, J., H. White and M. Wuyts. *Fundability and Sustainability: Import Support Aid to Tanzania.* Stockholm: SIDA, 1993.

Forss, K. *Planning and Evaluation in Aid Organizations.* Stockholm: Stockholm School of Economics, 1985.

Hanak, E. and M. Loft. "Danish Development Assistance to Tanzania and Kenya, 1962-85: Its Impact to Agricultural Development", in U. Leie (ed): *Aid to African Agriculture Lessons From Two Decades of Donor Experience.* N.p.:The Johns Hopkins University Press, 1991, pp. 168-231.

Havnevik K. J."Aid Cooperation- What Kind of Partnership? Experiences with Technical Assistance to Tanzania East Africa", *Forum for Development Studies,* No. 2, 1992, pp. 163-180.

Kipokola, J. P. "Aid Conditionality in Tanzania", paper presented to a Workshop on New Forms of Programme Aid, Harare, 1995.

Netherlands Development Co-operation. *Tanzania Evaluation of the Netherlands Development Programme with Tanzania.* The Hague: Ministry of Foreign Affairs, 1994.

Riddel, R. *Foreign Aid Reconsidered.* London: ODI James Currey, 1987.

Van Arkadie, B. *Public Sector Accountability and Competence - Tanzania.* Dar es Salaam: Mimeo, 1994.

World Bank, 1996. *World Bank Development Report,* Washington D.C.

Chapter **3**

Changing Aid
Relationships in Tanzania?
(A Progress Report, Year-End 1997)

by Gerald K. Helleiner
Professor Emeritus
Department of Economics
University of Toronto

Changing Aid Relationships in Tanzania?

This paper is an amalgam of some of the remarks made by the author at an informal dinner for heads of Delegation preceding the Tanzania Consultative Group meeting in Dar es Salaam, December 10-11, 1997, and his concluding summary remarks after the discussion of the "Helleiner Report" during the meeting on December 11. (Royal Danish Ministry of Foreign Affairs, Report of the Group of independent Advisors on Development Cooperation Issues Between Tanzania and Its Aid Donors, June 1995).

In mid-1994 the relationships between the Government of Tanzania and its aid donors were tense. Donors were deeply concerned with what they perceived as fiscal mismanagement, corruption, and inadequate attention to democratic processes. The Government of Tanzania saw donors as inappropriately intrusive and demanding. To try to bridge the differences between the government and its aid donors, an independent group of advisors was appointed jointly by the Danish Ministry of Foreign Affairs and the Tanzania Ministry of Finance. The group conducted its work during 1994-1995, a period during which aid relationships deteriorated even further. Its report was presented in June 1995.

The "Helleiner Report", as it became known, focused upon the immediate need for fiscal and macroeconomic stabilisation and the need, as soon as possible after the multi-party elections, to develop significantly altered relationships between the government and the donors, and major improvements in Tanzanian economic management. The report called for a change in operational culture on the part of aid donors, to reduce the gap between their rhetoric regarding the need for "national ownership" and the reality; and a significant strengthening of Tanzania programme leadership and financial management capacity. It was clear, at the time of the writing of the report, that such "second generation" reforms, following successful macroeconomic stabilisation, would be more difficult to address, take longer, and involve more independent actors than stabilisation itself. And so they are proving to be.

After the successful conduct of the 1995 elections, the consolidation of the new Tanzanian Government, and the new agreement with the IMF (achieved in November 1996) the time was ripe for a concerted approach to the issues raised by the report on aid relationships in Tanzania. A donor-government workshop on the report, held in Dar es Salaam in January 1997, achieved a remarkable consensus on the common objectives in new aid relationships and a number of first steps to be taken. The agreed notes from that workshop (appended) describe agreement that a new partnership between the donors and the Government of Tanzania would imply "a radical change of rules and roles between the partners in development". The guiding principle would be that "Tanzania takes the lead" and that "Tanzania fully owns the development cooperation programmes in terms of planning, design, implementation, monitoring and evaluation".

At the same time that these developments were taking place in Tanzania, there was increasing emphasis on the importance of national ownership of African adjustment and development programmes at the international level, for instance, in the Development Assistance Committee (DAC) of the OECD, in the meetings of the Special Programme for Africa (SPA), and in the World Bank. National ownership was everywhere stressed both as an end in itself and because of its proven developmental effectiveness. Representative of the new rhetorical consensus at the international level, on partnership and ownership, was a statement by the Chairman of the DAC:

> "If donors believe in local ownership and participation, then they must seek to use channels and methods of co-operation that do not undermine those values. External support must avoid stifling or attempting to substitute for local initiative .... The principles of self reliance, local ownership and participation which underlie the partnership approach are inconsistent with the idea of conditions imposed by donors to coerce poor countries to do things they don't want to do in order to obtain resources they need. That view of conditionality was always of dubious value. Treating development co-operation as a partnership makes clear that it is obsolete."
>
> (OECD, Efforts and policies of the Members of the development assistance committee, 1995, page 7)

80

Against this vigorous statement of aspirations one must place the continuing reality of the limited changes in actual aid practice and indeed the scepticism, in some circles, as to the potential practical application of such statements of principle. "Partnership in development" is not, after all, a new idea. Indeed it was the title of the report of another independent international commission, initiated by Robert Macnamara, then of the World Bank, and chaired by my compatriot, Lester Pearson, which appeared in 1969.

At the time of the release of that report, a prominent Indian civil servant with experience in aid relationships commented:

"Unfortunately, the concept of a genuine partnership in development ... lacks credibility. There has never been any real sense of equality between donors and recipients even when they attend the same consortium meetings and sit around the same table in many other forums. For the recipient to be frank about the policies or attitudes of donors in a forum where aid is to be distributed is about as difficult as the proverbial passage of the camel through the eye of a needle. Criticism of donor policies, even when it comes from non-recipient, is seldom answered in the manner in which recipients are obliged to answer the most far-reaching criticism of their own policies. There are obviously two sets of rules ... A mere equality of opportunity in engaging in dialogue cannot establish parity in decision-making ... The doctrine of mutuality in monitorship or genuine partnership in development is impractical ..." (I. G. Patel in Barbara Ward et al., ed., *The Widening Gap*, Columbia University Press, 1971, page 305).

Evidently there is some question as to whether a new form of aid partnership is possible. Can the principles of ownership transfer be translated into operational realities? Tanzania and its aid donors are "out in front" in efforts to implement the new principles of partnership and they will be closely watched - in other African countries, in the official aid community, and in non-governmental organisations. The potential significance of the Tanzania experience in this regard is therefore far greater than merely the success in addressing the problems to which the Helleiner Report was originally addressed.

What are likely to be the most important blocks to progress? If I have learned anything in my years in development policy, it is that change always takes longer than initially expected. It will be important to maintain forward motion ... and to monitor progress carefully. I can see five main potential problem areas; the problems can arise on both sides of the aid relationship.

First, there may be some confusion or disagreement as to what exactly is meant by "ownership" of national programmes. During our consultations with donors we heard some remarkable views as to what particular individual thought ownership meant, e.g.

- "Ownership exists when they do what we want them to do but they do so voluntarily."
- "We want them to take ownership. Of course, they must do what we want. If not, they should get their money elsewhere."
- "We have to be realistic. Our taxpayers want to be sure their money is being used well. They want to know there's someone they can trust, a national of their own country, in charge."

None of these seem to be remotely close to what the Chairman of the DAC has in mind!

On the other extreme, there have been a few on the Tanzanian side who seem to assume that transfer of ownership amounts simply to turning over the money, with few further questions asked.

In the US Congress today and in many other conservative donor circles, transfer of ownership is seen as shorthand for increasing self-finance of programmes and thus declining aid flows.

If there is no agreement as to what national ownership actually means in practice, there are likely to be continuing problems in achieving it. It should not be so difficult to achieve such agreement - involving both responsibility on the part of recipients and real "transfer" on the part of donors. Our report and the agreed notes from the January meeting can, I believe, be the basis for such agreement. But all of the participants in the new partnership (and unfortunately they typically turn over at a fairly rapid rate) must understand what has been agreed.

Second, there is a continuing danger that immediate pressures and short-term needs overwhelm the agreed longer-term objectives. Both sides of the aid relationship are vulnerable to this difficulty. With the best will in the world, the relevant actors may feel it necessary to address urgent problems directly and thus to postpone resolution of the real and ongoing issues of ownership. This has, of course, been a major problem over the history of African aid relationships. Both sides must understand that there may be some short-run costs and risks as the longer-term objectives are more vigorously pursued. Any productive investment involves a "gestation period" in which there are no returns and indeed some costs. Real change does take some time.

Third, the recipient government may fail to establish those minimum administrative and political conditions, sufficient to establish its credibility within the donor community and its actual capacity to lead. Recipient governments may thus be incredible to donor governments who cannot fully trust their capacity to own or effectively implement their programmes. As aggregate aid flows decline, it appears likely that the donors will focus their assistance more selectively at the country level. The question then becomes whether Tanzania is to be one of the select. Is it worth betting on or not? This is obviously primarily a matter for Tanzanians. The Government of Tanzania must continue to act so as to inspire confidence and trust.

Fourth, and to some degree a subcategory of the previous point, the recipient government risks being "set up" for failure via over-optimistic forecasts and expectations, both on the part of donors and of the government itself. Assessments of prospective performance are invariably biased upwards. Performance targets are frequently too numerous, too onerous, and inappropriately phased. Development programmes can thus be overloaded and the government, having failed to reach the targets, is then labeled as "undeserving". It is incumbent upon both donors and recipients to try to be realistic, about the prospects for economic performance and for policy change, and to take adequate account of unforeseen contingencies. In this sphere the IMF and the World Bank have a major role.

Fifth and last, the normal bureaucratic incentives found within aid agencies may continue to overwhelm the new partnership objectives. Aid bureaucrats must move their money, meet their deadlines, and answer to their own political masters. Perhaps the greatest risk of all - and the greatest impediment to change - is that mere lip service will continue to be given to the "new partnership" objectives while business continues as usual; and the gap between ownership rhetoric (in Washington and Paris) and the reality of aid relationships (in Dar es Salaam) remains wide.

The discussion on ownership and partnership issues in the Tanzania context has already gone beyond the generalities to some specific first steps. It is for that reason that there are such strong hopes for the evolution of aid relationships in Tanzania. The discussion between donors and recipients on these and other issues, at the December 1997 CG meeting in Dar es Salaam, has been very open and frank. Such frank exchange, however difficult, can engender mutual trust; and it must continue - albeit with a little more relative attention to donor shortcomings. It has constituted and important validation of one of the principles declared, in the January 1997 workshop, as essential to the new relationships: "an open, mutual and transparent dialogue on all aspects of ongoing development cooperation activities". This "process" is itself part of the " product" of a new aid relationship. And I believe there is consensus that the location of this meeting in Dar es Salaam, rather than in Paris, has contributed to this happy outcome.

It was a major accomplishment, as I have said, to agree (at the January workshop) on certain specific next steps to be taken in pursuit of the agreed objectives. Specific undertakings of this kind have many advantages. First, they provide a "reality check" as to what exactly the parties to an agreement are actually agreeing upon. Second, when the specifics are addressed, it is possible to generate dialogue on concrete matters and thus negotiate any necessary compromises. Third, specifying the details can make explicit the areas in which experimentation is proposed and in which both sides acknowledge, in advance, that there may be some risks. Lastly, listing specifics permits a clearer process of monitoring and evaluation. In short, specifics are the route to the operationalisation of the new objectives of partnership and national ownership.

On the basis of the discussions at this Consultative Group meeting, I believe it is possible to categorise the fifteen agreed "first steps" according to the degree to which progress has been made. I have three categories.

In the first category are those steps which have, at least to some degree, already been taken and in which the next objective must be to sustain existing progress and to keep moving in the same direction. In this category I would place Tanzanian leadership in the preparation of its Policy Framework Paper (PFP) and the next Public Expenditure Review (item vii). The PFP has also evidently now been made publicly available and some discussion of its major issues has been initiated with representatives of the private sector and civil society, although it is not clear that such discussions where initiated in advance (item iv). Some significant progress has also been achieved in this meeting in respect of the declared aspiration to: integrate donor-government discussion of debt relief and aid commitments" and governmental integration of its resource plans to facilitate this (item v). Obviously, however, no progress has so far been achieved in the direction of integrating Paris Club discussions with CG discussions. Lastly, in this category, we are, by virtue of this assessment, in the process of undertaking the agreed stocktaking of progress at this CG meeting (item xv).

In the second category are steps that, to some degree, have been initiated but in which it would probably be premature to judge the degree of progress since they are still so much "in process". In this category I would include:

- The provision of information on aid flows, including those in technical assistance, in kind, etc. (Item i);
- The rationalisation of development expenditures and donor programmes in the light of government priorities, with orderly exit from non-core activities (item ii);
- The building of financial management and planning capacity in the Treasury and Planning Commission (item vi);
- The provision of relevant accounting information, ideas and material support for the strengthening of governmental management of projects (item x);
- A review and rationalisation of the number and frequency of meeting among donors and between government and donors (item xii);
- In the third category are steps with respect to which there has so far been little progress and where it should be possible to initiate immediate action. In my judgment, from the discussions of the past two days, there are two particularly high - priority steps in this category.
- The identification of one or two subsets of the social sectors for focused attention, both for the Government of Tanzania and the aid donors, as they develop improved aid coordination modalities (item iii); there has been much discussion here about new coordinated approaches in the education, health, and local government sectors, but it is not evident that the required Tanzanian "lead" or donor response has yet materialised sufficiently to permit a truly integrated approach to sector planning;
- The proposed review of the effectiveness of technical assistance, about which I have heard nothing in the past few days (item xiii); the review was to consider appropriate modalities for the integration of technical assistance into overall programmes, for more effective capacity-building; assessing the opportunity cost of technical assistance; and

ensuring that selection and management is a Tanzanian responsibility.

The other steps to be taken in this category are:

- the initiation of discussion of major issues relating to the PFP with the private sector and civil society (the second part of item iv);
- donor efforts to develop more standardised information, accounting and reporting systems (item viii);
- the study of previous experiences elsewhere in the transfer of ownership or where there was greater recipient responsibility and longer-term donor commitments, such as in Eritrea (item ix).

It goes without saying that some mechanism for continued follow-up on all of these steps would also be appropriate and my understanding is that the CG Chairman has undertaken to put one in place.

In the third category, you may have noticed that two items have been omitted - those relating to improved project management (item xi) and to follow-up committees in Dar es Salaam, responsible for overseeing implementation of the agreement (item xiv). Needless to say, I consider the latter local follow-up to be critically important. I have not placed these into the previous categories because, frankly, I am not too clear as to what has been done on these fronts.

One might add some further agreed "next steps" that emanate from this meeting, for instance:

- the greater involvement of local non-governmental organisations in Tanzanian planning and discussions of policy; and
- the development of agreed practices with respect to donor "topping up" of local salaries.

All in all, I believe that both the Government of Tanzania and the donors can be proud of their progress thus far. At this point, the important priority is to look forward - at the possibilities and the implementation of agreements - rather than backward at previous failures and/or misunderstandings. Again, I believe that the frank and open dialogue accomplished at this meeting in Dar es Salaam augurs well for building the mutual trust upon which a new aid relationship based upon national ownership and partnership can be created. What you are working to accomplish here is important to all of Africa. Let me wish you every success with it in the coming year.

Appendix

Agreed notes from the Workshop on the Report of the Group of Independent Advisors on Development Co-operation Issues Between Tanzania and Its Aid Donors, Dar es Salaam January 1997

Preamble

Representatives of the donor community met with representatives of the Government of Tanzania, in Dar es Salaam on 14-15 January 1997, to discuss the Report of the Group of Independent Advisors on Development Co-operation Issues between Tanzania and its Aid Donors. The list of participants is attached.

The meeting agreed on the principles of a new development partnership to guide future co-operation between donors and Tanzania, a partnership that is effective, sustainable and beneficial to both sides.

1. It was agreed that a new partnership should be based on the following fundamental elements:

a) a solid Tanzanian policy platform in the context of the government's formulation of a vision for the future;

b) continuous and intensified Tanzanian efforts toward democratisation, at central and local levels, the upholding of human rights, freedom of the media, popular participation and gender equality;

c) strict Tanzanian adherence to its stated objectives to combat corruption, and further sustain good governance, and increase transparency in government;

d) achievement of macroeconomic stability and increased domestic resource mobilisation;

e) continuing reassessment of the role of the government, focusing on core functions, and inviting civic society and the private sector to shoulder increased responsibilities and roles.

2. The partnership should aim at sustaining assistance levels in the short and medium term. The long-term objective should be to replace traditional development assistance with other forms of bilateral co-operation.

3. A new donor - Tanzania development partnership implies a radical change of rules and roles between the partners in development:

a) Tanzania takes the lead in strengthening and building on existing institutional and other capacities in formulating visions, policies, programmes and projects; the guiding principle is that Tanzania fully owns the development co-operation programmes in terms of planning, design, implementation, monitoring and evaluation.

b) Tanzania ultimately takes full responsibility and accountability for the programmes and resources provided, and their results.

c) The participating partners always maintain an open, mutual and transparent dialogue on all aspects of on going development co-operation activities.

d) All activities agreed upon should be implemented on the basis of shared financing where the Tanzanian share successively increases over time. Dates for completion or termination should be agreed upon at the outset. The non-Tanzanian partners should be willing to make long-term financial commitments.

e) The partnership furthermore implies a willingness to move as quickly as possible towards providing budgetary support to sector investment programmes, based upon clear and consolidated Tanzanian sector policies and plans.

f) The development partnership should only comprise activities which are given priority by Tanzania and which are included in the development plans. The aim is that financing of these activities should be reflected in the development budget, ensuring completeness of budget information, as well as better monitoring of actual expenditures and disbursements. The development partnership should be demand-based and not driven by external partners.

4.   It was agreed that the new development partnership should enhance Tanzanian human capacity. To this end, it should increase allocation to the social sectors and national ownership. There was also agreement that the ultimate goal in changing the relationship between Tanzania and the donor countries should be to move away from traditional donor-recipient roles towards a broader relationship based on mutual long term interest and interdependence. Particular effort should be made to pursue a gender-mainstreaming approach in this enhancement process.

5.   As a first step towards initiation of this new donor-Tanzania partnership, the meeting agreed to the following:

(i)   In the interest of openness and transparency, as well as effective GoT aid management, concentrated effort should be made to gather/provide information on actual and planned aid flows to Tanzania including funds directed to entities other than the central government, including technical assistance and "in kind" expenditure, and to continue doing so on an on-going basis. This will permit complete resource budgeting in Tanzanian planning. Aid donors should provide such information or estimates to the best of their ability when asked. Responsibility for asking, and creation of an appropriate data frame, rests with the GoT.

(ii) Prioritisation and rationalisation of donor assistance - The government is currently severely over-committed in its support to development activities. Donors should support the government in its review of the development budget, aiming at prioritising and rationalising development expenditures in line with available resources. Donors should carefully review their expenditures and programmes in the light of the new principles and government priorities and seek orderly exit from non-core activities in consultation with government.

(iii) To test and develop aid co-ordination modalities and Tanzanian Government leadership, one or two subsets of the social sectors should be identified for focused attention (primary education? Primary health?). A review of the experience should be conducted after an appropriate period, say two years from its start.

(iv) In the interest of transparency and public understanding and participation, the most recent Policy Framework Paper (PFP) should be made publicly available. The government should initiate discussion on major issues relating to the next PFP with representatives of the private sector and civil society.

(v) In the interest of improved overall planning, resource mobilisation, and reduced administrative costs, efforts should be made to integrate donor-government discussion of debt relief and aid commitments. The Government of Tanzania should develop its own integrated resource plans to facilitate this.

(vi) Every effort should immediately be made by the government, with donor support, to build financial management and planning capacity in the Treasury and Planning Commission.

(vii) Tanzania should firmly take the lead in preparation of the next PFP and future Public Expenditure Reviews, with support from donors only in such a manner as to ensure Tanzanian control over the process.

(viii) To reduce the administrative burden on the government, renewed efforts should be undertaken within the donor community to develop more standardised information, accounting and reporting systems. Donors should in any case accept increased responsibility for converting available Tanzanian information into the forms required in their own current individual systems of accounting and reporting.

(ix) In order to learn from previous experiences in the transfer of ownership, the partners should undertake detailed analysis of the effectiveness of aid-financed projects, programmes and technical assistance in Africa that were characterised by high recipient responsibility and longer-term donor commitments.

(x) Increased transfer of resource management to Tanzania is dependent upon increased Tanzanian capacity to manage and account for such resources. Donors should collaborate with the Ministry of Finance in enhancing this capacity by providing all relevant information on their own accounting requirements, by providing ideas and material support for strengthening government mechanisms and, as capacity increases and to the extent possible, by increasingly transferring management of project resources to the Government of Tanzania.

(xi) Mainstreaming of project management - The existence of parallel implementation and staffing arrangements for projects has seriously undermined Tanzanian ownership, accountability, and capacity. As a first step towards "mainstreaming" of project management, CSD will prepare, in consultation with donors, a circular providing instructions on management responsibilities and staffing arrangements for projects administered by the Civil Service. Donors, in this regard, should finalise their report on project staff remuneration and use it as the basis for their joint consultations with CSD.

(xii) In principle, considering the high demand on the capacity of the government machinery and administration, the modalities of aid co-ordination should not add unnecessary demands to the already overstretched capacity. Therefore, the number and frequency of co-ordination meeting with the donors and between the government and donors should be reviewed and rationalised to ensure effectiveness and remove undesirable duplication.

(xiii) The effectiveness of technical assistance (TA) should be so as to:

- establish appropriate modalities for integrating TA in the overall human resources endowment available;
- institute modalities for effective capacity building and enhance the capacity-building role of TA;
- enhance complementarity between TA and local human resource utilisation and development;
- enable the opportunity cost of TA to be considered explicitly by all the partners;
- ensure that selection and management of TA is the responsibility of GoT.

(xiv) Modalities for follow-up of workshop recommendations - Each of these recommendations require specific follow-up. Follow-up should be included in the agenda of the next meeting of both the Inter-Ministerial Technical Committee and the Donor Assistance Group in Dar es Salaam (local DAC). Both of these groups should nominate representatives to a joint sub-committee which should be responsible for overseeing implementation of the recommendations and appropriately reporting to both the IMTC and DAC.

(xv) The development partners should undertake a formal stocktaking of progress on all of these fronts at the next CG meeting.

Chapter 4

Changing Aid
Relationships in Tanzania?
December 1997 through March 1999

Progress in Aid Relationships in Tanzania

by Gerald K. Helleiner
Professor Emeritus
Department of Economics
University of Toronto

Progress in Aid Relationships in Tanzania

Thanks and Acknowledgements

I have been honoured and pleased to be invited back by the Government of the United Republic of Tanzania to assess the progress made in aid relationships in recent years, and again to be supported in my work by the Royal Danish Ministry of Foreign Affairs. It has given me profound pleasure to work with the dedicated officials of the Government and the donor community, and with representatives of business, labour and the NGO community on a task to which they all obviously attach great importance. In all of the embassies, Government offices and homes I have visited in connection with this assignment, and in all of the many meetings and "working" meals to which I have been invited for further consultations, I have received complete cooperation and support and, most importantly, the true compliment of free, honest and frank exchange of information and impressions. There exists a long list of all those to whom I have spoken in connection with this assignment (which can be made available to anyone interested).

I should nevertheless like to thank all those who have taken the time to speak to me, provide me with relevant material (both before and during my stay in Tanzania), and otherwise make my job easier. Above all, I have been firmly and comprehensively supported, from start to finish of my 17 - day stay in Tanzania, by the Royal Danish Embassy in Dar es Salaam, most particularly by Ambassador Peter Lysbolt Hansen, who not only arranged my complex schedules and responded to my every request, but also acted as a most gracious and generous host throughout my stay. Those who most deserve thanks among his extremely competent staff are his ever-adaptable and hardworking secretary, Ms. Razia Haroon, and my driver, Mr. Peter Ndemu. For general support and record-keeping, I must thank my personal assistant throughout my stay in Tanzania, Dr. Longinus Rutasitara of the Department of Economics, University of Dar es Salaam. Lastly, I must record my deep thanks to the trusted friend, Mr. Johannes Zutt, who, although under other pressures himself, voluntarily gave up the better part of two days to type successive drafts of what eventually materialised as this report.

Lastly, I must emphasise that the views expressed in this report are entirely my own, not those of either the Government of Tanzania or the Royal Danish Government, and I accept total responsibility for them.

Gerald K. Helleiner
Dar es Salaam
23 March 1999

1. INTRODUCTION

The terms of reference for my report were clearly defined (Appendix D and they did not include a review of the economic performance of the United Republic of Tanzania. It is nonetheless important to record that the macroeconomic context for the changing aid relationship which I am mandated to analyse is a relatively healthy one, one which places Tanzania among the ranks of Africa's "good performers". Despite setbacks from weather shocks and commodity price declines, GDP growth in recent years has been maintained, albeit at modest levels (3.6% real growth in 1998), and the non-food inflation rate has dropped to 6.1% in January 1999, according to the Bank of Tanzania. Headline inflation dropped to 9.1%, the first time that single-digit inflation has been attained in Tanzania in 23 years. With the prospect of new mineral production coming on stream, further external debt relief, continued official development assistance, and the hope of "normal" weather, Tanzania now seems poised for significantly expanded growth by the year 2000 and thereafter. Moreover, its achievements have been realised simultaneously with a complex shift to multiparty democracy.

It is now widely recognised that aid is far more likely to be effective when there is macroeconomic stability in the aid-receiving country, and its overall economic policies are not egregiously "off-track". A major remaining condition for aid effectiveness, increasingly acknowledged both in the analytical literature and in the rhetoric of the international aid community, is true national ownership of its own development programmes. Tanzania's problems remain enormous and daunting. Still, there are hopeful signs that aid may be about to become a much more important contributor to successful assault upon them rather than, as sometimes in the past, generating doubtful effects; for all the key conditions for maximum aid effectiveness are now at last falling into place in Tanzania, including the national ownership on which I have been asked, among other matters, to assess progress.

Aid relationships have made remarkable progress since the 1995 Helleiner Report, particularly under the new Government headed by President Benjamin William Mkapa. The "agreed notes" of January 1997 spelt out the terms of a possible new mode of Government - donor interaction (Appendix II) and some specific first steps toward that end. Despite some continuing difficulties and disappointments my overall assessment is that significant progress has been made along the new path offered by that agreement. Both the aid donors (including multilateral agencies as well as bilateral donors) and the Government appear, by and large, sincerely to have striven to act in the spirit of the new agreement, and they have, in fact, as I shall outline below, achieved considerable forward motion. They have done so against a backdrop of continuing progress in the international rhetoric of "partnership", "dialogue", "ownership", etc. in "aid relationships" within the OECD, the World Bank, the UN system and even, to some extent, the IMF. In my view, the Government of Tanzania and the donor community have managed, against heavy odds, to overcome pockets of initial scepticism and have actually converted quite a lot of that general rhetoric into specific country - level practice.

The objective of this review was "to gather information and impressions on progress achieved towards implementing the agreed actions". In particular, it was asked to assess progress towards: "establishing GoT leadership in conceiving and executing development programmes in close partnership with its external partners and local stakeholders;

Changing attitudes and adoption of flexibility in procedures for aid delivery and utilisation consistent with a new partnership approach;

Improved aid coordination and integration of aid resources in agreed expenditure frame/development priorities;

Greater transparency in aid delivery on the part of donors and accountability for its use on the part of the GoT;

Reduction in malfeasance and adoption of explicit measures to rid the country of corruptive practices;

Greater involvement of the local stakeholders outside of the Government in development management; and

Overcoming such other obstacles to good relationships between the Government of Tanzania and the donors as have been identified either in the Helleiner Report or in the reviewer's subsequent investigations".

In the following sections, I address each of these aspects of progress in turn. Thereafter I turn to the specifics of the agreed "next steps" in improving the relationship between the Government and the donors as contained in the "agreed notes" of January 1997 and the discussions in the Consultative Group (CG) meeting of

December 1997. There is some inevitable overlap in the subject matter of these two sections but not so much, I hope as to cause the reader great distress.

2. MAJOR ISSUES - PROGRESS REPORT
2.1 Establishing Government of Tanzania Leadership

The Government of Tanzania has moved significantly towards the assertion and establishment of a degree of leadership over its development programmes which, while still not complete, would hardly have been conceivable when the Helleiner Report was originally written (in 1995). This leadership has been particularly strengthened in the 1998-99 period, since the last CG meeting, and it has been broadly supported both by the bilateral and multilateral donor community, which appears to be unanimous in its positive assessment of this development. The change is manifest most dramatically in the sphere of macroeconomic management, wherein the Government has led the preparation of the Policy Framework Paper (PFP), and effectively involved both the line Ministries and the entire cabinet in the process. When presented and finally successfully negotiated with the IMF, the PFP had taken much longer than usual to complete but, for the first time, its full Tanzanian ownership was clear to all. World Bank staffs were highly supportive of this new PFP process and backed the effort to ensure maximum Tanzanian ownership to the fullest extent one could imagine. (The important precedent of the mandate for a senior resident bank official to work closely and, more important, freely with his own Government seems to be generating a fruitful outcome).

Timetables did not appear to permit much, if any, involvement of non - governmental actors in the PFP process this year, but it is planned to involve them more fully in the process next year. This will require an earlier start, and the Government has accepted this necessity. The World Bank has offered its full support for such a move for consultative, and therefore probably lengthier, process of PFP development in the interest of ensuring broader Tanzanian ownership in the coming year.

Further impressive evidence of new Government leadership in the macroeconomic sphere has been its role, again fully supported by the World Bank and the bilateral donors, in the Public Expenditure Review (PER), a process which is itself closely linked to future fiscal and broader development planning and particularly to the Medium-Term Expenditure Framework (MTEF). Chaired by the Government and drawing on a wide range of independent (and local) consultants, a PER Working Group (composed of professionals from government, the donor community, academic institutions and consulting firms) planned, evaluated and effectively used the available budget and related material to assess experience, draw lessons, and make appropriate projections in a highly professional manner. The PER process in Tanzania, led by the Government, provides a model for others of the high potential for social gain, from professional cooperation at the local (country) level when appropriately led.

Frankly, it is surprising to me that the international donor community does not yet appear to have noticed the remarkable transfer of leadership and ownership at the macroeconomic level in Tanzania; but I do not doubt that they soon will. The IMF with its tradition of tighter timetables and shorter time horizons appears to have greater inherent difficulties in adjusting to the lengthier processes implicit in greater and broader local ownership, and the short - term adaptation and flexibility in timetables it may entail. So far the potential for consequent frictions has not been completely successfully contained; in part, such frictions may derive from the personalities. But there is likely to be more to it than just that.

The contrast in the approaches of the two institutions (the World Bank and the IMF) to the ownership issue, revealed in Tanzania and elsewhere, together with the long - standing problems that the IMF has had in converting itself from a monetary (short - term and crisis - oriented) institution to a more development-oriented one (both problems highlighted in the 1997 External Review of the ESAF, led by Dr. Kwesi Botchwey) have profound implications for the current discussions of an improved international financial architecture. When ESAF/IDA - eligible countries eventually overcome macroeconomic crises, which often have to be addressed in an atmosphere of urgency, even emergency, they have to shift to greater relative emphasis on the structural and governance reforms which require participation, extensive consultation, and political processes. The "next generation" of reforms requires greater care on the part of external sources of funds to ensure full local ownership, greater donor flexibility as to their pace and even their detailed makeup, and more time. The development banks (the World

Bank and the regional development banks) are much better suited to a supportive role at this stage than the IMF, which might then do best to retreat to the role of specialised supplier of technical assistance rather than continuing to assume the key role of condition - setter and "gatekeeper" for the (larger) supplies of external finance. At some point, donors may wish to reconsider the degree to which they trigger their own disbursements to overly short-term IMF-determined judgments.

At the sectoral level, the record is unfortunately not yet so positive, or indeed even so clear. Certainly the Government has taken formal leadership over the health and education sectors and, with a little more controversy, the roads sector. Vigorous efforts have been launched, under Government leadership, to establish sector-wide programmes in these three sectors. In each case, a Government-donor working group has been established and, at the time of writing, is still trying to work out appropriate modalities for donor coordination and cooperation; and each is chaired by the Government.

Prospects for success in the new sector-wide approaches are somewhat "muddied" by the simultaneous, speedy and fairly massive Local Government reform in which many of the traditional functions of the central line Ministries are being decentralised to the district level. (On this subject, see also Section 2 (iii)). The precise modalities for future interaction between the line Ministries and the soon-to-be more powerful district councils still have to be worked out. Again, there is a Government - chaired working group on local government reform on which the donors sit with Tanzanian officials to try to work out the operational modalities of the new district-level delivery systems for basic services. The transfer of the Ministry of Regional Administration and Local Government, which now carries responsibility for overseeing the new district council functions, to Dodoma has unfortunately complicated the effort to achieve a smooth transition to the new system, and achieve the necessary coordination both with other Ministries and with donors.

Only a very few donors have had direct experience working with district-level authorities. Most are somewhat nervous about the capacity to manage the proposed extra funds at the district level and would prefer a more cautious approach to local government reform. An external appraisal of the Government's Local Government Reform plans recommended at least a six-month delay in the startup of the actual transfer of funds and greater preparatory training and efforts to coordinate with relevant Ministries in the meantime. Further thought should be directed to the possibilities for breaking up the different elements of decentralisation of responsibilities into component parts and carefully sequencing them so as to minimise the risks of disrupting delivery of basic services and/or overwhelming financial management capacities at the district level. The appraisal team called for a phased transfer of responsibilities over a three to five year period. It also called for the return of the Ministry responsible for Local Government to Dar es Salaam. Government of Tanzania political leadership in this sphere is quite clear, but in this case, professionals, whether foreign or local, are almost unanimously advocating greater caution about the pace and modalities of change and questioning the quality of some of advice upon which the Government appears to be relying.

In the roads sector, there has been disagreement between donors and the Government over the appropriate use of funds (maintenance vs. construction) and appropriate control systems. Elements of the Government's original plans, some even already passed by parliament, were, in effect, vetoed by the donors who were expected to fund some of them. An accommodation was fairly quickly reached - an example in which "partnership" probably produced a superior outcome but - the original Government leadership and ownership was fairly clearly quickly over-ridden by the funders. Even in this case, however, the Government now appears to be in full control of the (altered) arrangements for funding and managing the road system. Frank and open dialogue did not result in a turnover to donors, but rather to a more transparent and accountable road management system.

It has been quite striking to me that there now seems to be so little attention directed to the agricultural sector and its problems, either in donor circles or in the central economic management departments of the Government (to which I was principally directed in this assignment). Agriculture remains the backbone of the Tanzanian economy, the rural scene is still where the bulk of the people are and where the bulk of the poverty remains. After the admirable push towards improved delivery of health, education, water and (trunk) roads, it may be time to shift more relative donor and Government attention back to the continuing multi-faceted problems of agricultural and rural production and marketing again.

2.2 Changing donor attitudes and Aid Delivery Systems

There is absolutely no doubt that aid donor attitudes have changed in the past two years, and most are quick to say so. The donors regularly state their appreciation of the greater Government acceptance of responsibility and leadership that they now experience. At the same time Government personnel speak of the much greater degree to which they are "listened to". In working groups, committees, and in general, there now seems to be much more genuine donor dialogue with Government, based on mutual respect, and, perhaps at least partly in consequence, a greater excitement and mood of optimism about Tanzanian prospects which, only a few years ago, were considerably more gloomy. A certain self-confidence has returned to the Government of Tanzania at all levels.

But have donor practices actually changed? Yes and no. Some donors are bound by the same constraints and interests as they always have been. But among most of the major donors there have been some important changes. Among them are:

- Active participation in regular sector-wide meetings under Government leadership.

- Contributions to "basket funds" in the health, education, roads and local government reform sectors, in support of mutually agreed common objectives.

- Contributions to the Multilateral Debt Fund, which was first suggested by the Government of Tanzania at the last CG.

- Significantly reduced numbers of expatriate technical assistance personnel and/or shifts in such personnel from line to facilitating or advisory functions.

- Increased use of local personnel and materials (although I have no firm aggregate data on this matter).

The sector-wide approach to donor-recipient relationships, which is in the process of a serious launch in Tanzania, has profound implications for traditional donor practices. It requires a shift away from the traditional directly-controlled project approach, the timely provision of complete information (actual and planned, and including directly funded activities), increased emphasis on sector-wide policies (and the capacity and willingness for frank dialogue on them), the turning over of some budgetary control and procurement functions to a "foreign" authority and, above all, the acceptance of local Government leadership and ultimate responsibility for the sector programme. It should not be surprising if some donor agencies are cautious, slow and reluctant or unable to make the shift. And its efficacy is still being tested. Still, under the terms of the agreement of January 1997, the donors and the Government have come rather a long way in quite a short space of time. There is no reason to doubt that this progress will continue, provided that periodic evaluations ensure that agreed objectives are being met. Progress in the implementation of this form of increased Tanzanian ownership is bound to be slower than that observed in the "first-round" changes at the macro level.

There are also grounds for modest optimism about some more general changes in donor attitudes and practices. Firstly, new approaches to the Highly-Indebted Poor Countries (HIPCs) from the international financial institutions and their major shareholder may both speed Tanzania's eligibility for the HIPC debt relief initiative and improve whatever terms it receives. (If this occurs, however, there should be no rush to dismantle the MDF. The last year has demonstrated the extreme fragility of debt sustainability projections in such HIPC beneficiary countries as Uganda and Bolivia). Secondly, there is also optimistic talk in the OECD about finally presenting a proposed text for untying ODA to the Least Developed Countries at the OECD DAC High Level Meeting in 1999.

2.3 Improved Aid Coordination and Integration of Aid within Tanzania's Development Priorities

As already noted Tanzanian leadership and altered donor attitudes have genuinely changed the aspirations of all parties. In the still nascent sector-wide programmes in health, education and, in a refurbished fashion, the road-sector, Government-donor joint working groups meet regularly (weekly in the case of the health sector) under Government chairmanship. This has encouraged increased mutual understanding and joint efforts to overcome constraints on individual donors so that all may be able to contribute whatever they have to contribute within the context of the overall effort within this sector. It is too soon to say how effective these arrangements will be in practice but there is evident mutual goodwill and progress in the appropriate direction. Neither of the expert appraisals of the health and education sectors had been completed at the time of writing. My general impression is that the health group was better directed and had a clearer sense of direction than the education group, but this is based on fairly superficial evidence.

As noted above, both health and education sector-wide planning has been somewhat disrupted by the major Local Government Reform launched by the Government of Tanzania since the last CG meeting. It calls for major decentralisation of previously central governmental activity to the district level in three (two-year) phases beginning with 35 districts in mid -1999. This throws the planned activities of the central line Ministries into a state of some uncertainty and will require detailed consultation and agreement between them, their sector-wide working groups, and the Ministry of Regional Administration and Local Government which, unfortunately for easy consultation, is now located in Dodoma. (The shift to Dodoma has generated a major imbalance in the composition of the Local Government Reform - donor working group which meets in Dar es Salaam and is therefore dominated by donors; the working group is chaired by a Dar es Salaam-based Ministry official who does not carry the authority of his senior colleagues based in Dodoma). The result is considerable potential for waste of time, energy, and materials already invested by the central organs (Ministries and donors), and high anxiety about the potential of the district authorities to manage their greatly increased responsibilities and the finances that come with them. Despite their doubts and their clear preference for a more gradual and selective transitional process, donors have nonetheless supported these Government initiatives, including even the provision of some basket funding to help prepare the reforms.

In the road sector, where an earlier "integrated road programme" proved inappropriately organised and managed, the donor community took a very strong stand against the Government's plans and insisted on a "ring-fenced" Road Fund, based on fuel levies, with the bulk of this Fund earmarked for maintenance and an independent Road Agency with major private-sector presence in (and chairmanship of) its Board. Following this decisive donor response to what they perceived as another impending road sector crisis, the Government adopted the donor suggestions and, with some key personnel changes, close Government-donor cooperation has resumed and a better-organised and integrated road programme has emerged, with widespread optimism as to its prospects.

Planning and financing for rural and feeder roads is not covered, however, in this new set of arrangements and again there is uncertainty and anxiety as to the capacity of the district councils to fulfill the needs in this sphere. Here, as in the social sectors, very few donors - however willing they may be - have had direct experience interacting with governmental authorities at the district level. Donors' capacities to integrate their activities in a coordinated fashion into the development priorities manifested in a new highly decentralised Tanzanian governmental system is likely to be significantly less than at present. They are generally aware of this threat to their current modes of working together under Tanzanian leadership, and many are worried about it.

2.4 Greater Transparency in Aid Delivery on the Part of Donors and Accountability for Its Use on the Part of the Government

In response to requests for information from the Ministry of Finance, aid donors in Tanzania are willing to respond as best they can. Smaller donors lack the staff to provide rapid or detailed information. There is general willingness to supply information both on technical assistance and other direct funding that does not pass through the Tanzanian budget. There are complaints, however, about the degree of detail requested and the frequency of such requests. The quarterly Government-donor meetings do not yield the project data that can contribute to the universally accessible and up-to-date information system for which many had hoped. The Ministry is in the process of building a significantly improved financial data storage and retrieval system using the latest software and equipment. Very few donors have found the extra resources required to fit their own data into the format requested by the Government and some question the need for and/or use to be made of such data and/or resent the sometimes uncoordinated data requests emanating from different wings of the Government.

It is obviously far more difficult to provide data for the future such as is required for full Tanzanian budget and resource planning than for past disbursements, since the former are often subject to changing donor policies, audit requirements, evaluations, and the like. Again, the direction of change in aid transparency is appropriate, though progress has still been relatively limited. It is a tragedy that significant sums already allocated for important developmental purposes are not spent because of delays or shortfalls in reporting or audits, sometimes audits in the donor capitals, and/or the shortage of required counterpart funds.

There has been important strengthening of Treasury budget management in the past two years. In parliament's Public Accounts Committee (chaired by the Deputy Leader of the Opposition parties) and the Auditor General's Report, there are still, however, unacceptable levels of unaccounted for or inappropriate use of public funds. Strenuous efforts to strengthen budgetary and financial controls must continue. In the meantime, Tanzania continues to operate a "cash budget", in which expenditures are confined strictly to revenues received. At some point, to facilitate the reordering of priorities, these "frozen" allocations will have to be loosened in the interest of new priorities for growth and development. The Government has made a firm commitment (to the IMF, among others) that this will not occur prematurely and, in particular, that elections in the year 2000 will not affect the planned continuation of the cash budget approach. There is consensus that the Ministry of Finance requires greater strength in the Policy Analysis Division, and steps have been initiated, with the support of the Civil Service Department, to ensure that it gets it.

Thus Tanzania "aid management" has undoubtedly progressed but there is still room for much improvement and in particular, fuller use of available funds. It is disappointing when donors are unable to deliver on their promises or their "estimates" but intolerable when donor funds fall short of expectations because of deficiencies in Tanzania's own aid management system; and some of this is still going on.

2.5 Reduction of Malfeasance and Adoption of Explicit Measures to Rid the Country of Corruptive Practices

It is obviously impossible for a report of this kind to add much value to the continuing discussion of malfeasance and corruption in Tanzania. There still appears to be constant complaint on the part of the media, the donors and, so it is said, the "person on the street" that petty corruption is still rife. The Minister of Health, while launching further anti-corruption measures in March virtually admitted that the situation was not yet showing much sign of improvement in his own sector. Talk about corruption at high levels of the Government also continues, although now it seems to have shifted somewhat from current malfeasance to the debate over appropriate punishment for misdeeds of the past.

The corruption phenomenon is not unique to Tanzania and is certainly common among surrounding countries and others at similar levels of income. Much more distinctive of Tanzania is the open discussion of the issue in the Warioba Report and its aftermath, including a further Warioba-led consultancy to the President which reported on the progress of measures taken to combat corruption between the time of his original report and the present (early 1999). Such comprehensive, honest and open reporting is almost unique in the developing world.

There can be no doubt that the President has personally waged a vigorous campaign of reforms and public education against any corruption that may be taking place during his own term in office, the details of which are summarised in a Presidential paper of February 1999. This paper calls attention not only to the difficulties of corruption-proofing the key organs of Government (revenue and procurement authorities, police, courts, etc.), but also to the high financial costs of doing so.

It is extremely difficult to assess the overall impact, if any of the anti-corruption measures so for taken. It is fairly certain, however, that when Transparency International recently rated Tanzania, on the basis of a survey (of uncertain quality) of public perceptions (resident and expatriate), as among the three or four most corrupt countries in the world, it primarily reflected the more widespread and open discussion of the issue in Tanzania than elsewhere and thereby dealt a severe blow not only to the morale of those engaged in the struggle against corruption but also to the Government's efforts to encourage foreign private investment in Tanzania.

Donors might do more to assist the Government in its anti-corruption efforts by:
- If not yet done, ratifying and enforcing the OECD Convention on Combating Bribery of Foreign Public Officials in International Business Transactions (agreed in December 1997);
- Assisting Government revenue and monetary authorities in the monitoring of unusual private international financial

transactions, for which software has been developed in connection with the international battle against money laundering and economic crime;

Consideration of a "sector-wide" approach, under Government leadership, to meet the financial needs described in the recent Presidential matter on the Fight against Corruption. Obviously, in this sphere care must be taken that Tanzanian-ownership is complete; non-governmental involvement in monitoring and evaluation may be very helpful within any such approach.

2.6 Greater Involvement of the Local Stakeholders, Outside of the Government in Development Management

Very little has been attempted on this front as yet. In the preparation of next year's PFP, the Government has declared its intention of involving non-governmental stakeholders actively in public debate over its content. There are hopes that the decentralisation of governmental activities implicit in the Local Government Reform will facilitate the involvement of the local citizenry in decisions relating directly to their welfare. As long as there remains no agreed set of regulations for the registration of non-governmental organisations (NGOs) (and their nature has turned out to be politically controversial), local NGOs find it difficult, they say, to make their voices heard. The shift of location of the CG meeting from Dar es Salaam to Paris obviously constitutes a major immediate setback to their efforts, individual and collective, to be informed and to be heard on policy questions relating to Government relations with donors.

2.7 Overcoming other Obstacles to good Relationships Between the Government and the Donors

(a) In my judgment, the most immediate source of unnecessary friction between the donor community as a whole and the Government of Tanzania, which has not been mentioned yet, is the plan to locate the next CG meeting in Paris rather than in Dar es Salaam. The next meeting of the CG after the Government-donor agreement to radically alter the aid relationship took place, as recommended in the January 1997, in Dar es Salaam (in December 1997); and it was generally regarded as highly successful. The President and the entire cabinet took part, making it possible for its members to better understand the overall relationship between the donors and the Government, to reply in detail to donor questions and debate their concerns, and generally to share the responsibility for and ownership of the Tanzanian programme, rather than leaving it to the Minister of Finance and a few officials to try to represent them in a far-off capital. Business, trade unions and NGOs were also provided with an opportunity to interact with the donor community, and the vigorous local press and media gave it full coverage. The relatively transparent and participatory character of the 1997 Dar es Salaam CG seemed an apt and highly visible symbol of the radical change in aid relationships upon which the donors and the Government have embarked. In addition, it also both saved the Government some money and earned Tanzania some tourist revenues.

Regrettably, all of this success and the important attendant sense of deeper and more widespread Tanzanian ownership appears to have been forgotten or played down in the preparation of the 1999 CG meeting which, over strenuous and continued Tanzanian objection, is planned to be held-in Paris. The donor community voted (narrowly) for a meeting in Paris rather than Dar es Salaam, arguing (among other things) that they could not otherwise guarantee the attendance of senior officials from their national capitals (although the multilateral agencies and at least one donor country are likely to be represented in Paris by their Dar es Salaam representatives anyway). In a "partnership" agreement, one would normally then declare the vote to be a tie: one vote for the donors, one vote for the Government. When donors are purportedly working hard to transfer a sense of ownership to the Government, when the previous CG meeting so obviously and effectively furthered that objective, and when the Government (which formally requested the meeting) felt strongly that the 1999 meeting should also be held in Dar es Salaam, the eventual decision to hold the meeting in Paris must be seen as a major setback to the entire initiative toward a new aid relationship. If the President is forced to travel to Paris to participate in what he properly considers a highly important meeting for his country's future, as he is considering doing, after having vigorously argued for a Dar es Salaam location, the negative symbolism will be unfortunate. One should not thereafter expect the Government to regard the purported "ownership" transfer quite as seriously. This is a matter on which the Government feels strongly. In the future, CG meetings should be held in Dar es Salaam.

(b) A recurrent issue in my discussions with individual donors, though not really an "obstacle" to good relationships, was the question of whether the average Tanzanian felt involved in any serious way with the Government's reform programmes, the progress it had already achieved or, in particular, its vision for the future. There seems, at present, to be some uncertainty as to the precise status of the latest draft of the "Vision 2025" documents. The President and at least one of his cabinet ministers have recently referred to it in public speeches but it is not clear whether it already represents official policy. There does not seem to have been any official "launch" of the statement. Nor is it easy for the average Tanzanian to see it, either in English or in Swahili. Its length and general character are, in any case, not conducive to easy digestion by the mass population. Many wonder, as one put it, "Whatever became of Vision 2025?"

As agreed in the original Helleiner Report, the broad population of the United Republic of Tanzania would benefit greatly from the provision of a widely disseminated and popularised statement, perhaps even in greatly simplified (even slogan) terms, of where the Government is trying to lead them. Now that the Government has more clearly taken over the leadership of its programme, and its overall economic performance and prospects are much stronger than they were, its pronouncements of its vision for Tanzania's future can carry much more credibility than before. How to undertake all this is, of course, a matter of political judgment. But it seems to many, both Tanzanians and donors, that the time has come for the Government to do much more with the Vision 2025 document upon which so much time and energy has been expended.

3. DETAILED AGREED FIRST STEP—PROGRESS REPORT

Let me now address each of the 18 agreed first steps. Fifteen are recorded in the "Agreed Notes" circulated after the Government-donor meeting of January 1997; one, that relating to the location of the next CG meeting, was inadvertently dropped from the circulated version. In my summary remarks at the CG meeting of December 1997, I added a further two to which I heard no objection. To facilitate understanding of my overall judgment on each point, I have assigned a (letter) grade to the progress made on each point (A is excellent; F is failure).

(i) "In the interest of openness and transparency, as well as effective GoT aid management, concentrated effort should

111

be made to gather/provide information on actual and planned aid flows to Tanzania including funds directed to entities other than the central government, including technical assistance and 'in kind' expenditure, and to continue doing so on an on-going basis. This will permit complete resource budgeting in Tanzania planning. Aid donors should provide such information or estimates to the best of their ability when asked. Responsibility for asking, and creation of an appropriate data frame, rests with GoT".

As noted above, progress has been made within the constraints of available resources and knowledge. No doubt further progress will be made as data systems improve and an appropriately simplified and standardised format is developed by the Government so as to permit it to collect only that information that it most requires and cut back on repetitive or extraneous requests. Grade: B.

(ii) "Prioritisation and rationalisation of donor assistance - The government is currently severely over committed in its support to development activities. Donors should support the government in its review of the development budget, aiming at prioritising and rationalising development expenditures in line with available resources. Donors should carefully review their expenditures and programmes in light of the new principles and government priorities and seek orderly exit from non-core activities in consultation, with government".

Prioritisation and rationalisation has taken place, and the number of projects has been significantly reduced via a collaborative PER process. With only a few exceptions, donors have reviewed their activities in the light of Tanzania's priorities and have eased their pressure to include their own projects within the Tanzanian "core". There does seem to remain some donor uncertainty, at least as expressed to me, as to what exactly the remaining "core" or "super-core" projects now are. Most donors seem willing to remain within whatever framework the Government of Tanzania sets. There are plans, led by the World Bank, to replace its own country assistance strategy with a comprehensive, coordinated and cooperative external donor country assistance strategy which it would be actively encouraging, though not necessarily leading. Grade: B+.

(iii) "To test and develop aid coordination modalities and Tanzania Government leadership, one or two subsets of the social sectors should be identified for focused attention (primary education? primary health?). A review of the experience should be conducted after an appropriate period, say two years from the start".

The Government has tried to do considerably more than promised in this sphere by focusing attention on the entire education and health sectors, rather than adopting a more narrowly focussed approach. It may have tried to do too much too fast, and the situation is further complicated by the Local Government Reform, which is probably being pushed at too rapid a pace for the wellbeing and efficiency of these sectors. Appraisals are already under way—of the proposals rather than the experience. Grade: B+.

(iv) "In the interest of transparency and public understanding and participation, the most recent Policy Framework Paper (PFP) should be made publicly available. The government should initiate discussion of major issues relating to the next PFP with representatives of the private sector and civil society".

The previous PFP was made publicly available at the end of the December 1997 CG meeting in Dar es Salaam. The current one will also be made publicly available although it is not clear exactly when. Its contents were more widely discussed within government than ever before. Time did not permit more public discussion this time but it has been promised for the next time. Grade: A.

(v) "In the interest of improved overall planning, resource mobilisation, and reduced administrative costs, efforts should be made to integrate donor-government discussion of debt relief and aid commitments. The Government of Tanzania should develop its own integrated resource plans to facilitate this".

Substantial progress has been made on this front via the successful initiation of the Multilateral Debt Fund after it was requested by the Government of Tanzania at the last CG. Positive donor responses were very quickly received. The reports to the MDF group admirably integrate the discussion of debt issues (including the buyback of unguaranteed commercial debt at about 12 cents on the dollar, with donor support) with general macroeconomic reporting. Grade: A.

(vi) "Every effort should immediately be made by the government, with donor support, to build financial management and planning capacity in the Treasury and Planning Commission".

As noted above, much has been done but much remains to be done. Grade: B.

(vii) "Tanzania should firmly take the lead in preparation of the next PFP and future Public Expenditure Reviews, with support from donors only in such a manner as to ensure Tanzanian control over the process".

This has been done with great success. I believe Government practice in these areas probably now leads Africa. Grade: A+.

(viii) "To reduce the administrative burden on the government, renewed efforts should be-undertaken within the donor community to develop more standardised information, accounting and reporting systems. Donors should in any case accept increased responsibility for converting available Tanzanian information into the forms required in their own current individual systems of accounting and reporting".

Very few concrete results have been reported in this area. One large donor noted that the time of one of its staff is now devoted exclusively to the task of conversion of Tanzanian data into its own data reporting system. No effort at standardisation has apparently been made by the DAC in this area. Grade: D.

(ix) "In order to learn from previous experiences in the transfer of ownership, the partners should undertake detailed analysis of the effectiveness of aid-financed projects, programmes and technical assistance in Africa that were characterised by high recipient responsibility and long-term donor commitments".

This has not been addressed and is now probably better left to the research communities in the international financial institutions (who might be specifically asked to undertake research in this area), universities, and development research organisations. Grade: F.

(x) "Increased transfer of resource management to Tanzania is dependent upon increased Tanzanian capacity to manage

114

and account for such resources. Donors should collaborate with the Ministry of Finance in enhancing this capacity by providing all relevant information on their own accounting requirements, by providing ideas and material support for strengthening government mechanisms and, as capacity increases and to the extent possible, by increasingly transferring management of project resources to the Government of Tanzania".

Strenuous efforts have been made and continue to be made to strengthen the budget management, accounting and audit capacities within both the Government and the Tanzanian private sector. New needs have now been added at the district level in connection with the Local Government Reform programme. Improvement can obviously only be achieved gradually. Adequate salaries and other incentives must be part of the strengthening programme. Major progress can be reported at the level of the central organs of the Government, notably in the Treasury and the Tanzania Revenue Authority, much of it buttressed by focused technical assistance. It will be critically important to prevent slippage from what has already been achieved and to continue the current forward momentum which has been accompanied not only by improved performance but also by higher morale as competence and self-confidence grows. Grade: B.

(xi) "Mainstreaming of project management—The existence of parallel implementation and staffing arrangements for projects has seriously undermined Tanzanian ownership, accountability, and capacity. As a first step towards 'mainstreaming' of project management, CSD will prepare, in consultation with donors, a circular providing instructions on management responsibilities and staffing arrangements for projects administered by Civil Service. Donors, in this regard, should finalise their report on project staff remuneration and use it as the basis of their consultations with CSD".

This set of recommendations has been overtaken, to some degree, by other events. It is possible to report, however, that in the spirit of the overall agreement, most donors say that they have been attempting to phase down their parallel staffing and implementation agreements and plan to bring them into line with overall Tanzanian programmes and reformed salary structures as soon as they are in place. A great deal now depends on the early implementation by the Civil Service Department of the revised pay structure, the proposed innovations in performance-related remuneration, and of course, the response from those most affected. Donors have not made any attempt yet, so far as I am aware, to harmonise their own remuneration and allowance arrangements for the local personnel employed in their projects on either a temporary or a permanent basis. In the current context, it is appropriate for the Government's Civil Service Department to take the lead and to continue the effort to "mainstream" more donor projects and other activities under Government leadership. There would nevertheless be some sense in a formal discussion among donors themselves concerning their pay and related practices as they relate to their Tanzanian employees. Grade: C+.

(xii) "In principle, considering the high demand on the capacity of the government machinery and administration, the modalities of aid coordination should not add unnecessary demands to the already overstretched capacity. Therefore, the number and frequency of coordination meetings with the donors and between the government and donors should be reviewed and rationalised to ensure effectiveness and remove undesirable duplication".

It has not been possible for me to conduct a systematic study of this question. It is my distinct impression, however, that the number of coordination meetings between donors and senior Government officials has not declined, and indeed has probably increased, in connection with the initiation of sector-wide approaches to aid management.

The new commitment to quarterly meetings between the Government and the entire donor community constitutes an important innovation, however, and they appear so far to be functioning reasonably well, serving as a forum for the reporting of general progress and problems and the mutual exchange of ideas and concerns. Generally, however, Government representation at these meetings has been at a more senior (Permanent Secretary) level than that of the donors; if this imbalance in the level of representation persists, the prospect of regular Government-donor dialogue among "equals" will diminish, and this potentially very useful instrument for the assertion of Tanzanian leadership, the encouragement of frank and open dialogue between the Government and donors, and reduction in the number of Government-donor meetings cannot succeed. Senior-level donor participation in these meetings is an important signal to the Government of the seriousness of donor commitment to the new aid relationship. Every effort should be made to make this instrument of cooperation work—with serious joint attention devoted to appropriate agenda for each meeting and with full representation at appropriately senior levels. Grade: C.

(xiii)" The effectiveness of technical assistance (TA) should be so as to:

- Establish appropriate modalities for integrating TA in the overall human resources endowment available in the country;
- Institute modalities for effective capacity building and enhancing the capacity - building role of TA;
- Enhance complementarity between TA and local human resource utilisation and development;
- Enable the opportunity cost of TA to be considered explicitly by all the partners;
- Ensure that selection and management of TA is the responsibility of " GoT".

Roughly 30% of all aid disbursed on behalf of Tanzania is at present estimated to be in the form of technical assistance. (The estimated average for sub-Saharan Africa is about 40%.) Most major aid donors now supply information on technical assistance disbursements to the Government when requested. In the view of most independent analysts of the economic value of these expenditures (which typically do not flow through the Government budget system), they are not all wisely spent. They contain large elements that are not cost-effective so far as Tanzania's development is concerned and frequently serve other (donor) objectives. These expenditures, unless "additional", as in cases where there is no country frame (e.g. Finland), clearly can carry a very high opportunity cost for Tanzania, in that these funds could otherwise be used for more productive purposes.

Many donors have been reducing technical assistance expenditures in response to negative assessments of their value, spending more of these allocations on local firms or individuals rather than importing expensive (and often ill informed) external expertise. Some have also actively involved the Government in the selection of technical assistance personnel. All of these reforms and innovations are positive and in the spirit of the agreement.

It remains true, however, that much of the technical assistance expenditure in Tanzania is perceived by the Government as an unnecessarily wasteful use of scarce aid resources, contributing little either to local human resource use (employment) or to capacity-building which together are among the Government's top priorities. Because foreign technical assistants usually do not offer first loyalty to Tanzania, the Government also often perceives them as positively detrimental to the development of local Ownership of Tanzanian programmes, which is ostensibly the object of the new aid relationship to promote. Despite some progress, technical assistance expenditures therefore remain among the most sensitive issues in the jointly agreed effort to transfer ownership to Tanzanians. Needless to say, analogous issues arise between international NGOs and Tanzanian civil society. Grade: C.

(xiv) " Modalities for follow-up of Workshop recommendation - Each of these recommendations requires specific follow-up. Follow-up should be included in the agenda of the next meeting of both the Inter-Ministerial Technical Committee and the Donor Assistance Group, Dar es Salaam (local DAC). Both of these groups should nominate representatives to a joint subcommittee which should be responsible for overseeing implementation of the recommendations and appropriately reporting to both the IMTC and DAC".

As has been seen above, the follow-up to these recommendations has been taken very seriously. It is epitomised by this report, which has been requested by the Government and financed by the Royal Danish Government. Grade: A.

(xv) The development partners should undertake a formal stock-taking of progress on all of these fronts at next CG meeting".

The commissioning of this report by the Ministry of Finance and its funding by the Royal Danish Government and the complete cooperation of virtually all the donors, large and small, multilateral and bilateral, is evidence of the seriousness of this commitment. (At an earlier stage - at the last CG meeting - it was the World Bank that invited my active participation as an independent monitor, despite the fact that our original report had singled it out for particular criticism, and it has continued to be highly supportive of my work in the current undertaking).

I believe that, if all parties find it useful to continue, it is now time for the Government of Tanzania and the donors to attempt to systematise the process of independence of emerging aid relationships and identification of new or potential problems in them. How best to do this, if at all, might best be decided in the new spirit of national ownership by the Government of Tanzania following discussion at one of the new quarterly Government-donor meetings. At the same time, there is much to be said for greater donor transparency in their own individual self-evaluations and even for some greater efforts toward formal collective self-evaluations, either in the aggregate or at the sectoral level, at regular (or even irregular) intervals in between CG meetings. Grade: A.

(xvi) Meetings of the Consultative Group should take place in Dar es Salaam rather than in Paris.

This issue was thoroughly discussed in Section II (vii). Grade: A+ for 1997; F for 1999.

(xvii) Greater involvement of local non-governmental organizations in Tanzanian planning and discussions of policy.

Since this topic was addressed in Section II, there is no need for repetition here. Grade: C.

(xviii) The development of agreed practices with respect to donor "topping up" of local salaries.

The subject of public sector pay reform and capacity-building (and retention) in key governmental positions remains absolutely fundamental to the sustainability of the Tanzanian development effort and the efficacy of its ownership programmes. Donor policies continue to be at variance one with another, creating confusion, inequity, and inefficiency. "High wage islands", such as those of the Tanzania Revenue Authority and the Central Bank, can be important instruments for improvement in government performance in selected key sectors, but there are obviously early limits to the extension of their use. A variety of other devices have been employed to attract and retain high quality-personnel in key positions, some of them highly inefficient (e.g. the plethora of allowances related to conferences, workshops and seminars, all of them completely uncoordinated).

The Government's (CSD) plans for public sector pay reform and its draft guidelines for rationalisation of donor compensation schemes offer hope for a generally sound medium-term solution. Pending the raising of domestic revenues to the higher levels expected to be realised through growth and tax reforms over the next three to five years, donor contributions to a "basket fund" created for that purpose would make it possible to raise the relevant key salaries much earlier without doing violence to the Government budget. This fund could gradually be tapered down to zero over the relevant time period and, provided that donors maintained discipline in the form of self-denying ordinances against "undercover" topping up (including subsidised housing), such an innovation could go far toward restoration of appropriate incentives and order in the upper levels of the civil service salary structure. The proposals for an incentive component, basing increases upon performance, are of course also very welcome and will help donors to resist the temptation to return to the practices they have formally foresworn. Grade: B.

120

4. SUMMARY

The Government of Tanzania has moved significantly toward the assertion and establishment of a degree of leadership over its development programmes which, while still not complete, would hardly have been conceivable when the Helleiner Report was originally written (in 1995). The change is manifest most dramatically in the sphere of macroeconomic management, wherein the Government has led the preparation of the Policy Framework Paper (PFP) and effectively involved both the line Ministries and the entire cabinet in the process. World Bank staffs were highly supportive of this new PFP process and backed the effort to ensure maximum Tanzanian ownership to the fullest extent one could imagine.

Further impressive evidence of new Government leadership in the macroeconomic sphere has been its role, again fully supported by the World Bank and the bilateral donors, in the Public Expenditure Review (PER), process which is itself closely linked to future fiscal and broader development planning and particularly to the Medium-Term Expenditure Framework (MTEF).

The IMF, with its traditions of tighter timetables and shorter time horizons, appears to have greater inherent difficulties in adjusting to the lengthier processes implicit in greater and broader local ownership, and the short-term adaptation and flexibility in timetables it may entail.

The "next generation" of reforms requires greater care on the part of external sources of funds to ensure full local ownership, greater donor flexibility as to their pace and even their detailed makeup, and more time. The development banks (the World Bank and the regional development banks) are much better suited to a supportive role at this stage than the IMF, which would then probably do best simply to retreat to the role of specialised supplier of technical assistance rather than continuing to play the key role of condition-setter and "gatekeeper" for the (larger) suppliers of external finance. At some point, donors may wish to reconsider the degree to which they trigger their own disbursements to overly short-term IMF-determined judgments.

At the sectoral level, the record is unfortunately not yet so positive, or indeed even so clear. Prospects for success in the new sector-wide approaches are somewhat 'muddied "by the simultaneous, speedy and fairly massive, Local Government Reform, in which many of the traditional functions of the central line Ministries are being decentralised to the district level. Government of Tanzania political leadership in this sphere is quite clear; but, in this case, professionals are almost unanimously advocating greater caution about the pace and modalities of change.

There is absolutely doubt that aid donor attitudes have changed in the past two years. In working groups committees, and in general, there now seems to be much more genuine donor dialogue with the Government, based on mutual respect. Among most of the major donors there have been some important changes. Among them are:

- Active participation in regular sector-wide meetings under Government Leadership.
- Contributions to "basket funds" in the health, education, roads and local Government reform sectors, in support of mutually agreed common objectives.
- Contributions to the Multilateral Debt Fund.
- Significantly reduced numbers of expatriate technical assistance personnel and/or shifts in such personnel from line to facilitating or advisory functions.
- Increased use of local personnel and materials.

The sector-wide approach to donor-recipient relationships, which is in the process of a serious launch in Tanzania, has profound implications for traditional donor practices. It should not be surprising if some donor agencies are cautious, slow, and reluctant or unable to make the shift. Still, under the terms of the agreement of January 1997, the donors and the Government have come rather a long way in quite a short space of time. Progress in the implementation of this form of increased Tanzanian ownership is bound to be slower than that observed in the "first round" changes at the macro level.

It is too soon to say how effective these new arrangements will be in practice but there is evident mutual good will and progress in the appropriate direction. Health and education sector-wide planning has been somewhat disrupted by the major Local Government Reform launched by the Government of Tanzania since the last CG meeting. Despite their doubts and their clear preference for a more gradual and selective transitional process, donors have nonetheless supported these Government initiatives, including even the provision of some basket funding, to help prepare the reforms.

In response to requests for information from the Ministry of Finance, aid donors in Tanzania are willing to respond as best they can. There are complaints, however, about the degree of detail requested and the frequency of such requests. The Ministry is in the process of building a significantly improved financial data storage and retrieval system using the latest software and equipment. Again, the direction of change in aid transparency is appropriate, though progress has still been relatively limited.

There has been important strengthening of Treasury budget management in the past two years. There are still, however, unacceptable levels of unaccounted for or inappropriate use of public funds. Strenuous efforts to strengthen budgetary and financial controls must continue. Thus Tanzanian "aid management" has undoubtedly progressed but there is still room for much improvement and in particular, the fuller use of available funds.

There can be no doubt that the President has personally waged a vigorous campaign of reforms and public education against any corruption that may be taking place during his own term in office. It is extremely difficult to assess the overall impact, if any of the anti-corruption measures so far taken. Donors might do more to assist the Government in its anti-corruption efforts by:

- If not yet done, ratifying and enforcing the OECD Convention on Combating Bribery of Foreign Public Officials in International Business Transactions;

- Assisting Government revenue and monetary authorities in the monitoring of unusual private international business financial transactions;

- Consideration of a "sector-wide" approach, under Government leadership, to meet the financial needs described in the recent presidential paper on the Fight against Corruption.

In the preparation of next year's PFP, the Government has declared its intention of involving non-governmental stakeholders actively in public debate over its content. The shift of location of the CG meeting from Dar es Salaam to Paris obviously constitutes a major immediate setback to their efforts, individual and collective, to be informed and to be heard on policy questions relating to Government relations with donors.

The relatively transparent and participatory character of the 1997 Dar es Salaam CG meeting seemed an apt and highly visible symbol of the radical change in aid relations upon which the donors and the Government have embarked. In the future, CG meetings should be held in Dar es Salaam.

The time has come for the Government to do much more with the Vision 2025 document upon which so much time and energy has been expended.

The new commitment to quarterly meetings between the Government and the entire donor community constitutes an important innovation. Senior-level donor participation in these meetings is an important signal to the Government of the seriousness of donor commitment to the new aid relationship. Every effort should be made to make this instrument of cooperation work—with serious joint attention devoted to the appropriate agenda for each meeting and with full representation at appropriately senior levels.

Most major aid donors now supply information on technical assistance disbursements to the Government when requested. They contain large elements that are not cost-effective so far as Tanzanian development is concerned. Despite some progress, technical assistance expenditures therefore remain among the most sensitive issues in the jointly agreed effort to transfer ownership to Tanzanians.

If all parties find it useful to continue, it is now time for the Government of Tanzania and the donors to attempt to systematise the process of independent monitoring of emerging aid relationships and identification of new or potential problems in them. There is much to be said for greater donor transparency in their own individual self- evaluation and even for some greater efforts toward formal collective self-evaluations either in the aggregate or at the sectoral level, at regular (or even irregular) intervals in between CG meetings.

The subject of public sector pay reform and capacity building (and retention) in key governmental positions remains absolutely fundamental to the sustainability of the Tanzanian development effort and the efficacy of its ownership programmes. Donor policies continue to be at variance one with another creating confusion, inequity, and inefficiency. Donor contributions to a "basket fund" created for that purpose would make it possible to raise the relevant key salaries much earlier without doing violence to the Government budget.

Agreed Notes from the Workshop on the report of Group of Independent Advisors on development Co-operation Issues Between Tanzania and its Aid Donors, Dar es Salaam.

Preamble

Representatives of the donor community met with partnership of the Government of Tanzania in Dar es Salaam on 14-15 January 1997 to discuss the report of the Group of Independent Advisors on Development Co-operation Issues between Tanzania and its Aid Donors.

1. It was agreed that a new penmanship should be based on the following fundamental elements:

(a) Solid Tanzanian policy platform in the context of the government's formulation of a vision for the future;

(b) Continuous and intensified Tanzanian efforts toward democratisation, at central and local levels, the upholding of human rights, freedom of the media, popular participation and gender equality;

(c) Strict Tanzanian adherence to its stated objectives to combat corruption and further sustain good governance, and increase transparency in government;

(d) Achievement of macroeconomic stability and increase domestic resource mobilisation,

(e) Continuing reassessment of the role of the government, focusing on core functions, and inviting civic society under private sector to shoulder increased responsibilities and roles.

2. The partnership should aim at sustaining assistance levels in the short and medium term. The long - term objective should be to replace traditional development assistance with other forms of bilateral co-operation.

3. A new donor-Tanzania development partnership implies a radical change of rules and roles between the partners in development.

(a) Tanzania takes the lead in strengthening and building on existing institutional and other capacities in formulating visions, policies, programmes and projects; the guiding principle is that Tanzania fully owns the development co-operation programmes in terms of planning, design, implementation, monitoring and evaluation.

(b) Tanzania ultimately takes full responsibility of and accountability for the programmes and resources provided and their results.

(c) The participating partners always maintain an open, mutual and transparent dialogue on all aspects of on going development co-operation activities.

(d) All activities agreed upon should be implemented on the basis of shared financing where the Tanzanian share successively increases over time. Date for completion or termination should be agreed upon at the outset. The non-Tanzanian partners should be willing to make long term financial commitments.

(e) The partnership furthermore implies a willingness to move as quickly as possible towards providing budgetary support to sector investment programmes, based upon clear and consolidated Tanzania sector policies and plans.

(f) The development partnership should only comprise activities which are given priority by Tanzania and which are included in the development plans. The aim is that financing of these activities should be reflected in the development budget, ensuring completeness of budget information, as well as better monitoring of actual expenditures and disbursements. The development partnership should be demand based and not driven by external partners.

4.   It was agreed that the new development partnership should enhance Tanzanian human capacity. To this end, it should increase allocation to the social sectors and national ownership. There was also agreement that the ultimate goal in changing relationship between Tanzania and the donor countries should be to move away from traditional donor-recipient roles towards a broader relationship based on mutual long-term interest and interdependence. Particular effort should be made to pursue gender - mainstreaming approach in this enhancement process.

5.   As a first step towards initiation of these new donors–Tanzania partnership, the meeting agreed to the following:

(i) In the interest of openness and transparency, as well as effective GoT aid management, concentrated effort should be made to gather, provide information on actual and planned aid flows to Tanzania including funds directed to entities other than the central government; technical assistance and in kind expenditure and to continue doing so at an on-going basis. This will permit complete resource budgeting in Tanzania planning. Aid donors should provide such information or estimates to the best of their ability when asked. Responsibility for asking and creation of an appropriate data frame rest with the GoT.

(ii) Prioritisation and Rationalisation of Donor Assistance- the Government is currently severely over-committed in its support to development activities. Donors should support the government in its review of the development budget that aims at prioritising and rationalising development expenditures in line with available resources. Donors should carefully review their expenditure and programme in the light of the new principles and government priorities and seek orderly exit from non-core activities in consultation with government.

(iii) To test the development aid coordination modalities and Tanzanian Government leadership one or two subsets of social sector should be identified for focused attention (primary education? Primary health?). A review of the experience should be conducted after an appropriate period say two years from its start.

(iv) In the interest of transparency and public understanding and participation, the most recent Policy Framework Paper (PFP) should be made publicly available. The government should initiate discussion of major issues relating to the next PFP with representatives of the private sector and civil society.

(v) In the interest of improved overall planning, resource mobilisation, and reduced administrative costs, efforts should be made to integrate donor-government discussion of debt relief and aid commitments. The Government of Tanzania should develop its own integrated resource plans to facilitate this.

(vi) Every effort should immediately be made by the government, with donor support to build financial management and planning capacity in the Treasury and Planning Commission.

(vii) Tanzania should firmly take the lead in preparation of the next PFP and future Public Expenditure Review, with support from donors only in such a manner as to ensure Tanzanian control over the process.

(viii) To reduce the administrative burden on the government, renewed efforts should be undertaken within the donor community to develop more standardised information, accounting and reporting systems. Donors should in any case accept increased responsibility for converting available Tanzanian information into the forms required in their own current individual systems of accounting and reporting.

(ix) In order to learn from previous experiences in the transfer of ownership, the partners should undertake detailed analysis of the effectiveness of aid-financed projects, programmes and technical assistance in Africa that were characterised by high recipient responsibility and longer-term donor commitments.

(x) Increased transfer of resource management to Tanzania is dependent upon increased Tanzanian capacity to manage and account for such resources. Donors should collaborate with the Ministry of Finance in enhancing this capacity by providing all relevant information on their own accounting requirements, by providing ideas and material support for strengthening of government mechanisms and, as capacity increases and to the extent possible, by increasingly transferring management of project resources to the Government of Tanzania.

(xi) Mainstreaming of project management - Existence of parallel implementation and staffing arrangements for projects has seriously undermined Tanzanian ownership, accountability, and capacity. As a first step towards "main streaming" of project management, CSD will prepare, in consultation with donors, a circular providing instructions on management responsibilities and staffing arrangements for projects administered by Civil Service. Donors in this regard, will finalise their report on project staff remuneration and use as the basis of their joint consultations with CSD.

(xii) In principle, considering the high demand on the capacity of the government machinery and administration, the modalities of aid co-ordination should not add unnecessary demand on the already overstretched capacity. Therefore, the number and frequency of co-ordination meetings with the donors and between the government and donors should be reviewed and rationalised to ensure effectiveness and remove undesirable duplication.

(xiii) The effectiveness of Technical Assistance should be reviewed with a view to:

- Establish appropriate modalities of integrating TA in overall human resource endowment available in the country.
- Institute modalities for effective capacity building and enhancing the capacity building role of TA.
- Enhance complementarity between TA and local human resource utilisation and development.
- Enable the opportunity cost of TA to be considered especially by all the partners.
- Ensure that selection and management of TA is the responsibility of GoT.

(xiv) Modalities for follow up of Workshop recommendations - Each of these recommendations requires specific follow up. Follow up should be included in the agenda of the next meeting of both the Inter-Ministerial Technical Committees and Donor Assistance Group in Dar es Salaam (Local DAC). Both of these groups should nominate representatives, to a joint sub-committee which should be responsible for overseeing implementation for the recommendations and appropriately report to both the IMTC and DAC.

(xv) The development partners should undertake a formal stock taking of progress on all of these fronts at the next CG meeting Terms of Reference for Review of Implementation of Recommendations by the Helleiner Report.

TERMS OF REFERENCE FOR REVIEW OF IMPLEMENTATION OF RECOMMENDATIONS BY THE HELLEINER REPORT

1. INTRODUCTION

Two years have passed since the recommendations from the Helleiner Report (1996) were adopted for action at a joint Government of Tanzania (GoT)-Donors meeting held in Dar es Salaam, January 1997. The immediate objective of the recommendations was to normalise the relations between the GoT and its external partners which were severely strained during October 1994 - June 1995, following GoT's disclosure of large revenue losses due to malfeasance. The longer term recommendations from the report set out a more ambitious agenda for redefining the GoT-Donors relationships in the conception and management of development programmes as well as for creating greater transparency and accountability in aid delivery and utilisation.

The spirit behind the proposed "new relationship" was that of creating a partnership and local ownership in designing and executing development programmes. The report also recommended a broader definition of local ownership to include other stakeholders in the process of development management.

Most important among the issues arising from the above changes pertain to the redefinition of the relationship between the Tanzanian Government and its external partners in managing the development process; the way the government and its partners relate to the ultimate beneficiaries of development assistance i.e. the local communities; and the relationship between the government and the private sector. The meeting in January 1997 reached agreement on a redefinition of the relationship between the GoT and its donors. The agreement is in principle to have the GoT to take the lead in the formulation of a development vision, drawing up strategies for realising this vision and activity programming. Once effectively operational, the Forward and Rolling Plan and the related Medium Term Expenditure Frame will be the main guide to sectoral prioritisation and resource allocation. Adherence to this guide, and within it the sector strategies, is key to cultivating the leadership position of GoT. A necessary condition for success is strengthening the human and institutional capacities in the key policy and sectoral ministries as well as in the local governments. The degree to which the ongoing civil service reform and the local government reform programmes adopt this as its central theme should be investigated.

A further issue in the redefinition of this relationship pertains to raising the effectiveness of aid provided to Tanzania as well as its own resources in facilitating both sustained growth and reduction of poverty. All parties involved in the partnership are concerned that protracted periods of large volumes of external assistance have not brought about the anticipated reduction in abject poverty as about 50% of Tanzanians remain below the international poverty line of $1 a day. Tanzania is still dependent on aid. It is now broadly accepted that efforts to mobilise its own resources and to unleash local initiative in development is fundamental to sustained development. The shift in thinking is towards application of aid as an enabling means for self-help from the perspectives of both financial resources and local capabilities for development management. The application of 'empowerment or local ownership' and 'sustainability' are key in this shift of paradigm.

2. OBJECTIVES OF THE REVIEW

Although the process of change in the GoT-donor relationships envisaged in the Helleiner Report will take longer to complete, a passage of two years since the adoption of an action plan in January 1997 offers a reasonable basis to assess progress. This review therefore is intended to gather information and impressions on progress achieved to date towards implementing the agreed actions.

More specifically, the review will assess progress towards:

Establishing GoT leadership in conceiving and executing development programmes in close partnership with its external partners and local stakeholders; changing attitudes and adoption of flexibility in procedures for aid delivery and utilisation consistent with a new partnership approach; improved aid coordination and integration of aid resources in agreed expenditure frame/ development priorities; greater transparency in aid delivery on the part of donors and accountability for its use on the part of GoT; reduction in malfeasance and adoption of explicit measures to rid the country of corruptive practices; greater involvement of the local stakeholders outside of the Government in development management; overcoming such other obstacles to good relationships between the Government of Tanzania and the donors as have been identified either in the Helleiner Report or in the reviewer's subsequent investigations.

3. METHODOLOGY

The reviewer will make every effort to come up with an appropriate methodology to achieve the above objectives. The suggestions offered here are intended to provide inputs to the reviewer for developing such a method.

Information on progress towards the above objectives can be sought in two-broad approaches: a review of documentation on policy undertakings to effect the required changes, and interviewing the key participants in the process of development management. Some of the key policy documents and processes to be reviewed include the process of preparing the Policy Framework Paper; the process of Public Expenditure Review; Budget Guidelines and Forward - and Rolling Plan; the process and output from preparation of sector strategies (Health, Education, Water, Environment, Poverty Eradication Strategy, Roads and Agriculture): documentation on Quarterly Joint Review of policy implementation and coordination; the format of CG meetings: development of Vision 2025 for Tanzania, and the Local Government Reform Policy document which will govern the progress of devolution of responsibilities to local authorities. Most of documentation related to the above can be availed in advance of the field interviews.

Interviews with key participants would include all core policy ministries; a sample of sector ministries (e.g. for priority sectors); DAC donors group; sector-wide donor/GoT groups; Public Expenditure Review Working Group; Private Sector associations; cooperative and labour movements; and women's groups. In light of a major movement towards devolution of responsibility for-providing social service to Local Governments and communities, it will be opportune to hold interviews with Ministry of Regional Administration and Local Governments, the Association of Local Authorities of Tanzania and the joint GoT/donors Working Group on Local Government Reforms.

4. EXPECTED OUTPUT

Report of 10-15 pages to be presented to the CG meeting in the first half of 1999 highlighting main findings and recommendations for further actions. The report should be finalised at least 3 weeks before the CG meeting if at all possible in order to give sufficient time for prior distribution to CG meeting participants.

Presentation of the report by the Reviewer at the CG meeting

If the Reviewer sees a need to supplement the main findings and recommendations for further actions presented in the report to the CG meeting a more comprehensive report should be finalised before the end of June 1999.

5. TERMS OF SERVICE

Duration of the review:
a) Predations: 2 weeks
b) Visit to Tanzania: ° week
c) Participation in CG meeting: week
d) Report writing: 2 weeks

The remuneration of the Reviewer will be agreed directly with Danida, 2 weeks of local consultancy will be provided to the Reviewer.

Chapter **5**

Tanzania Assistance Strategy: Critical Issues

by Gerald K. Helleiner
Professor Emeritus
Department of Economics
University of Toronto

May 2000

Tanzania Assistance Strategy: Critical Issues

A great deal of time and effort, most of it contributed by the Government of Tanzania (GoT), has gone into the production of the draft Tanzania Assistance Strategy (TAS), a framework document to guide the promotion of local ownership and development-partnerships. For this we must all be most grateful. The production of this document in time for discussion at the 2000 CG meeting - marks a potentially important further step towards the development of a new set of relationships between aid donors and the GoT.

Obviously there are still many questions to be asked. My task is to address some of them and, where possible, offer some suggested answers. To my mind, the most important broad questions raised by the draft TAS are the following: (1) How far have we so far come in the process of building the desired new partnership between the GoT and the donors? (2) What is still missing from the TAS? (3) Is the process for developing it reflective of the objectives it ostensibly pursues?

1. HOW FAR HAVE WE COME?

The most striking feature of the draft TAS is that, after its ringing Introduction (pp. 1-2), it is not until the twenty-fourth page of its twenty-five pages of text that one discovers any further reference to donors. And what then appears, under the heading of "Undertaking by Development Partners", is quite brief and uninformative in its specifics* . The concluding section on monitoring is equally brief and uninformative.

Also of concern is the lack of clarity as to Tanzanian priorities among its proposed "actions" and "areas" for "the way forward". Their presentation does not always make it easy for potential donors to ascertain how the Government of Tanzania would like them to respond.

What one can say, then is that the GoT has taken the leadership in preparing a consultation draft. It is clearly now for the donors to offer a coordinated response. In doing so, they should concentrate their attention, I would urge, on (1) the adequacy of the TAS statements of priorities for their own (donor) decision-making purposes, and clarification of what they require in this regard, in order to put Tanzania "into the driver's seat", and (2) the crucial last two pages in the document - on donor undertakings and monitoring. Until they produce a constructive and detailed response on both points, we do not yet appear to have come too far. One must hope that the donor group, at least those donors most actively pushing for change, have not been idle while waiting for the GoT draft; and that they will be able fairly quickly to respond.

2. WHAT IS STILL MISSING? AND SOME SUGGESTIONS

Implicit in the previous section is my own view of what is still missing from the TAS. The draft TAS is comprehensive in its coverage of the GoT's intentions, even if details often remain to be filled in later, and the expenditure framework is still missing (at least from the April 13th draft made available to me). Unfortunately, GoT priorities among the many, many undertakings described are also less than entirely clear. Details, expenditure framework and priorities will undoubtedly emerge in the further consultations planned with donors. Ultimately donors will need to know the anticipated size of the overall programme and its major components; and, critically important, what is in the "top priority" list and what is not.

It is now for the donors to specify clearly what further priorities and details they require to be able practically to implement the TAS.

On the other hand, as implied above, the donor commitment side of the TAS is far less complete. In part, this may just be a phasing problem inherent in the process through which the GoT took prime responsibility for the first draft of the TAS. But some missing donor elements need quickly to be addressed. In particular, if the general donor commitments/undertakings described in paragraph 6.4 - all of which are excellent as far as they go - are to be translated into effective practice, systematic monitoring and evaluation of donor performance is required. (Tanzanian performance is, of course, already monitored closely by the IMF, World Bank and many bilateral donors. No doubt these monitoring activities can and should be done in a more coordinated and collaborative manner. But there is little need for further monitoring of Tanzanian performance). Only with balanced performance monitoring can there be genuine balance in the overall partnership (let alone GoT leadership). Donor monitoring must be consciously planned; and the modalities of donor performance monitoring belong in the TAS.

One could begin by a general agreement generally to monitor the donor "undertakings" in paragraph 6.4, as the TAS has done. But I think it would be more productive to be considerably more specific as to donor monitoring indicators and processes. Let me make some concrete suggestions in this regard, all of which carry implications for the donors' response to the current draft and for the contents of the next version of the TAS. I shall offer them in the context of the broader worldwide discussion of "best practice" in aid relationships.

3. SUGGESTIONS FOR DONOR PERFORMANCE MONITORING IN THE TAS
3.1 Compliance with Recipient Requests for Information

Aid donors around the world evidently felt little compunction to report to the governments of the countries in which they conduct their activities as to what exactly they are doing there, what they have done in the past or what they intend to do in the future, let alone to do so in harmonised categories or according to timetables (or, in some cases, even in a language) that might be most useful to the local authorities. In the relatively infrequent instances when national governments have asked donors to supply such information, they have typically pleaded inability to do so or have complained of the inordinate cost of attempting it. In consequence economic decision-making in the more aid-dependent of the low-income countries is severely constrained in terms of critical data. In the Tanzanian case, standardised data reporting and response to governmental requests for data appear still to be a problem for some.

The degree of donor compliance with recipient governmental requests for standardised and timely aid data should therefore be an important performance indicator for donors. Such compliance may depend upon the nature of the data request. Some donors may readily be able to supply some information but not all. Donor-recipient dialogue should be able to engender agreement as to what is most useful and feasible to supply. The GoT should make its priority data needs and their form and timing as clear as possible. The performance indicator may have to be fairly crude, e.g. a dichotomous (yes/no) measure for each donor, both for performance and for "best efforts".

3.2 Degree to which ODA Expenditures fall within Recipient Budgetary System

A common popular misconception about ODA is that it is all passed through a recipient government system, even through its budget. For better or for worse, however, this is typically not the case. High proportions of ODA expenditures are made directly to the suppliers of goods and services to aid agencies - private firms, NGOs, individuals. Some of these direct expenditures are made to nationals (firms, NGOs, individuals, sometimes local rather than national governments) of the recipient country; traditionally, more have gone to foreigners, notably from the donor country. In the latter case, these funds do not register in either the donor or recipient country's balance of payments statistics, except indirectly when/if the recipients spend some of them in the recipient country. Needless to say, decisions as to the uses and recipients of such "direct funds" are made exclusively by the donors.

In Tanzania, where efforts have been made to transfer "ownership" of development programmes from aid donors to the government, only 30 per cent of ODA was estimated to flow through the government budget in fiscal year 1999. (It is disappointing to learn (from unpublished sources) that the figure for fiscal year 2000 is unchanged). The proportion of each donor's ODA expenditure that finds its way into the national budget system is another reasonable performance indicator for donors; this should be inclusive of debt forgiveness and contributions to the multilateral debt servicing fund.

3.3 Integration and Coordination within National Plans and Priorities

A related issue is the degree to which donor projects and expenditures are coordinated and integrated into national and sectoral plans and/or recognise the declared priorities of recipient

140

governments. The clearest and simplest manifestation of donor willingness to coordinate their support and follow national leadership is through contributions to sectoral or cross-sector "basket funds", administered by recipient governments in accordance with objectives and priorities agreed with the contributing donors. Donor support of this kind should be reflected in the data on the share of ODA making its way through the recipients' budgetary systems. But donors may also consciously tailor their activities and projects to recipient priorities, whether national or sectoral, and/or attempt to coordinate their support, standardise their accounting and reporting systems, reduce transactions costs for recipients, etc. without going all the way to "basket fund" contributions (which some donors are constrained, by their own national legislation, from making). On the other hand, they may continue, as they have so often done in the past, to set their own agendas and "push" projects that are not high in the recipients' order of priorities.

Some attempt should be made to assess donor coordination and willingness to accept local priorities in a systematic way. To some degree, what transpires in this respect is the product of the recipient government's determination to take leadership. In this respect, the assessment might be considered as among the most important indicators of the success of the aspired-for partnership, transfer of leadership and achievement of local "ownership". Perhaps a quantitative (negative) indicator of this, if it is feasible, is the percentage of ODA commitments or expenditures, which appear to "stand alone", outside of agreed priorities or coordination systems.

3.4 Shortfalls from ODA Promises

Aid donor announcements and even formal commitments often bear little relationship to subsequent actual disbursements. There are many reasons for this: administrative delays; recipient failure to meet pre-stipulated donor conditions, e.g. on local cost co-financing; changed political or economic circumstances in either donor or recipient countries, etc. By no means all the fault for donor shortfalls (overspending does not often occur) rests with the donors. For effective policymaking, however, one must have reasonably accurate resource projections, on a year-by-year basis, and preferably for longer periods such as are covered by a medium-term expenditure framework (MTEF). It may be more important to have predictable and reliable resource inflows than to have large flows that are highly erratic and uncertain. There must be a presumption that, where general macroeconomic management remains sound, and particularly in the case of general or sectoral budget support, the primary responsibility for exceptionally large shortfalls rests with the relevant donors. Their actual disbursements should therefore be monitored in the context of their own prior commitments. Their shortfalls, individual and collective, should constitute another performance indicator. It would be useful as well to distinguish shortfalls according to whether they related to the 30 per cent of ODA appearing in the GoT budgetary system or to the 70 per cent which did not (see suggestion (3.2) above); or even to whether they related to the broader category of "integrated" activities (see suggestion (3.3) above) or not.

3.5 Compensatory and Contingency Financing

It is important to recognise the exceptional need for liquidity and contingency finance in the poorest and least developed countries. Their structures and size make them peculiarly vulnerable to "shocks" from weather, terms of trade and even (though this is less widely recognised) private capital flows. At the same time, their access to commercial bank finance is limited (and/or costly) and the opportunity cost of the holding of foreign exchange reserves is always high in poor countries. IMF funding availability or /short falls of the amounts required fully offset these countries' shocks. It is, in any case, even in the case of its "Compensatory and Contingency Finance Facility (CCFF)", not available without new conditions, and hence delays heavy transactions costs at a time of already increased pressures on policymakers' time and energies; the IMF thus can no longer be described as a source of increased "liquidity" even with respect to the limited funds it can provide.

Bilateral donors, who routinely disburse (collectively) far greater amounts in support of poor countries than the IMF or World Bank, could - if they chose - purposefully alter the time profile of their disbursements for budget or balance of payments support in response to individual recipient countries' shock-generated needs for liquidity. Such "compensatory" variability of donor flows would help to impart greater predictability to entire country programmes rather than merely to donor flows and this could be extremely helpful to recipient countries. Donors should devote greater attention to this potential stabilisation role. Those able to perform such a role should obviously be favourably recognised for doing so rather than recorded as offering unstable and unpredictable finance.

3.6 Tying of Procurement

The tying of aid has long been recognised as costly to recipients, particularly when it relates both to its use and to its procurement source. It is particularly costly to the poorest countries who are least likely to be able to respond to its potential costs by taking maximum advantage of fundability. Despite years of effort, OECD DAC members have still not been able collectively to agree to untie all aid to the least developed countries.

Another obvious donor performance indicator, then, is the percentage of ODA, which is provided, whether in project or programme form, on an untied basis with respect to country of procurement. Since some donors have been willing to permit local sourcing or sourcing in other poor countries, while retaining the tying requirement on any "external" expenditures, it would probably be best also to record the percentage of ODA for which such partial sourcing freedom exists. (Technical assistance/ cooperation raises so many further issues (see below) that measures of aid donor tying should be calculated exclusive of technical assistance/cooperation expenditures as well as in total.)

3.7 Role of Technical Assistance/Cooperation

Technical assistance/cooperation expenditures have played a major role in overall aid to the poorest countries. That role has been controversial and is highly politically sensitive. The emerging consensus among aid analysts is that, great as the need for technical expertise may be in most of the poorest countries, traditional technical assistance/cooperation activities have been signally ineffective in sheer cost-benefit terms. Expatriate expertise is frequently ill informed and/or insensitive to local realities; typically generates little domestic learning, memory or capacity-building, sometimes serves donor rather than development interests (including donor monitoring and control objectives); and is always extremely costly. As both developing countries and donors have shifted their emphasis (at least at the level of their rhetoric) to long-term capacity-building, the limitations of the traditional model of expatriate technical assistance have been increasingly recognised. The latest draft World Bank research report on African prospects states:

"... on balance, it is likely that [these] aid programs have weakened rather than strengthened capacity in Africa. Technical assistance has served to displace local expertise and even substitute for civil servants pulled away to administer aid-funded programs - precisely the opposite of the capacity building intentions of both donors and recipients".

Technical cooperation expenditures in Sub-Saharan Africa still amount to about $4 billions per year and about one-quarter of all bilateral assistance to the region. In some countries these expenditures account for 40 per cent of total ODA. Under the traditional modalities, these numbers are simply too high; and recipients resent their perceived opportunity costs.

Another suitable (negative) donor performance indicator could be the percentage of its aid which is spent upon donor-country tied technical assistance/cooperation. Although there are plenty of "useful" expatriates working in Tanzania, the presumption must be that this is not generally now a wise use of aid funds, particularly when it has not been requested, and that recipient freedom from procurement tying increases overall cost-effectiveness. Hence good donor performance means a low percentage devoted to tied technical assistance. One could imagine some positive indicator of contributions to long-term capacity-building as a complement to this somewhat "negative" indicator; but this would have to be somewhat subjective and hence more difficult to devise.

3.8 Qualitative Assessments of Ownership

On other dimensions of the aid relationship there might also have to be resort to more qualitative assessments, undertaken by independent evaluators, of individual and collective donor performance. In Tanzania, an independent assessor last year assigned letter grades to the collective performance of donors with respect to a variety of promises they had made regarding the transfer of "ownership" of development programmes (along with relevant commentary). (See also suggestion (3.12) below).

3.9 Time Horizon for ODA Commitments

Some attempt should be made to record systematically the degree to which donors have been able to make longer-term commitments, e.g. within the framework of an MTEF.

3.10 Humanitarian versus Development Assistance

Although the distinction between humanitarian aid and development assistance is sometimes difficult to make, it is critical to efforts to assess the developmental impact of ODA in the poorest countries. Analyses of the growth or investment effects of ODA, of which there have been so many, and about which there has been so much controversy, must make this distinction if they are to carry any credibility; and most do not. DAC publications already draw this distinction in their aggregate data for individual donors. It should therefore be quite feasible to report these useful specifics at the level of individual recipient countries. There should be no presumption as to which form of ODA is "better" in this effort to assess the information relevant to analysis of aid's impact.

3.11 Individual and Collective Donor Performance Indicators

All of these indicators should be recorded both for individual donors, or at least those accounting for significant ODA in Tanzania, and for the donor community as a whole.

3.12 Independence of Monitoring Authority

Fundamental to the credibility and effectiveness of any such performance monitoring is the independence of the evaluator(s). Neither the donors nor the Bretton Woods institutions can be trusted to be neutral and apolitical in their assessments of donor performance. Political influences may also bedevil the potential UN role in such activities. Still, the UNDP (or possibly UNCTAD) could serve as an appropriate and ongoing financier and organiser of independent assessments of donor performance via contracting with private individuals, teams of individuals ("panels"?), or consulting firms to provide these services. The production of the UNDP's annual Human Development Report is handled in this manner. So are many of the other research and technical cooperation activities of both UNDP and UNCTAD. Alternatively, the work could continue to be funded and contracted by individual (or groups of) "like-minded" donors. Whoever the financiers/organisers, it must be clear to all that the assessors retain absolute independence and that the contractors/donors carry zero responsibility for their conclusions. Tanzanian experience suggests that such procedures are entirely feasible. It is important to record agreement on the precise monitoring modalities in the TAS document.

3.13 Frequency of Performance Assessments

Since change in aid relationships is likely to take some time and since, in any case, every effort should be made by donors to reduce recipient transactions costs and take a longer view, the current one-year cycle for performance assessments of the aid relationship, as well as for the donor consultations associated with Consultative Group (CG) meetings is probably too short. The more balanced assessments of donor and recipient performance here recommended, and probably CG meetings themselves, need not take place so frequently. It could be worth experimenting with a two-year cycle for CG meetings. If CGs continues to be held every year, one should not attempt full-blown and balanced assessments of performance in the TAS more frequently than every other year (i.e. biennially).

4. PROCESS

Among the principal objects of the initiative that led to the TAS were the rationalisation of development activities, reduction of unnecessary duplication and cutbacks on the heavy transactions costs of dealing with so many external sources of funds. The process of producing the draft TAS ran parallel with many other GoT planning efforts - the preparation of the PRSP, a medium-term expenditure framework (MTEF), and an annual budget, not to speak of sectoral and district-level efforts at a less aggregated level. The TAS was not intended to make more work for the GoT or to duplicate its ongoing planning and budgetary exercises. On the contrary, it was to make life a little easier for the GoT. It was to complement the preparation of the PFP (now the PRSP) and the MTEF, not duplicate or draw scarce skilled personnel away from them. Pressed to prepare a TAS and without guidance from any prior experience with this task, the GoT interpreted what was required rather broadly and, in so doing, may have neglected the "assistance" issues narrowly defined. This may have led it into significant and undesirable overlap with the PRSP and other efforts and unnecessary extra work.

In the future, any unproductive duplication and waste of GoT effort should be avoided. Donors should make it clear to the GoT that they do not require any TAS document to contain the comprehensiveness of coverage of GoT intentions that appears in the present TAS draft. (The PRSP could usefully be appended to the TAS document.) The PRSP and the processes which create an agreed PRSP, the PER/MTEF process and other GoT documents should adequately inform donors as to the GoT's intentions. The TAS should focus its attention on assistance issues, including identification of the types and amounts of ODA that are most required (and, eventually, one hopes, who will provide them). The TAS initiative should be, as its introduction says, about an ongoing process of ODA rationalisation and coordination rather than production of a TAS document. The processes of the TAS initiative should be quite different from those creating the PRSP or the PER/MTEF. In particular, while the GoT must lead the TAS process, it would probably be efficient to involve donors in the making of commitments at an earlier stage, particularly those that had been planned – but remain general and/or thin - on "monitoring and evaluation" and "best-practice development cooperation". If donors had more specific early information on GoT priorities and priority areas for their assistance (and the forms in which it is most useful) they could make firm ODA commitments within the TAS framework more quickly and effectively.

Since a TAS has not been developed before, everyone involved is still " learning by doing". As donors now seek to respond to the draft TAS, they too may make mistakes. The most important requirement for the eventual success of the TAS initiative is that a spirit of mutual open-ness and trust be cultivated and maintained - and that the processes continue.